The Major Messages of the Minor Prophets

JOEL:
THE DAY OF THE LORD

AMOS:
THE RIGHTEOUSNESS OF GOD

OBADIAH:
DOOM UPON EDOM

By

CHARLES LEE FEINBERG, Th.D., Ph.D.

PROFESSOR OF SEMITICS AND OLD TESTAMENT
Dallas Theological Seminary, Dallas, Texas

Published by

AMERICAN BOARD OF MISSIONS TO THE JEWS, INC.
236 West Seventy-second Street
NEW YORK 23, N. Y

To
PAUL DAVID,
LOIS ANNE,
JOHN SAMUEL,
God's Gifts of Great Love,
This Volume Is Lovingly Dedicated
By
Their Father

AUTHOR'S PREFACE

THE articles incorporated in this volume, part of which have already appeared in the pages of *The Chosen People* and part of which remain to be published, are meant to form a volume uniform with the "Studies in Hosea" which have appeared in book form as *Hosea: God's Love for Israel*. The present work constitutes volume two in a series of five projected for all the minor prophets.

The purpose of the writer is the same in this volume as in the previous one; namely, to inculcate in Christian hearts from the Word of God a love for God's own people Israel, and to encourage the widespread preaching among them of the gospel of their Messiah, the Lord Jesus Christ.

The words that have come to us concerning encouragement and blessing received through these studies have led us to hope that God may make them a source of similar refreshing to a wider group of the Lord's people. If it be so, we shall give thanks to God.

Dallas, Texas   CHARLES L. FEINBERG.

CONTENTS

JOEL:
THE DAY OF THE LORD

Chapter I
THE LOCUST PLAGUE AND DAY OF JEHOVAH

The Prophet and His Times

JOEL, a name borne by many in the Old Testament, means "Jehovah is God." A few have suggested that this prophet was the son of the prophet Samuel (cf. 1 Samuel 8: 2), but the Scripture here is clear that the Joel of the prophecy was the son of Pethuel, of whom we know nothing further. In contrast to the fullness of detail given in relation to the life of the prophet Hosea, practically nothing is known of the personal history of Joel. From the prophecy itself we may gather that he was a prophet of Judah and that he probably prophesied in Jerusalem. Note the references to the sanctuary in Jerusalem in 1: 9, 13, 14; 2: 15. Joel was probably one of the earliest of the minor prophets. Compare the quotation of Joel 3: 16 in Amos 1: 2 and that of Joel 3: 18 in Amos 9: 13. The sins denounced by Amos and Hosea are not mentioned here, nor is the sin of idolatry touched upon at all. There is difference of opinion among students of the book as to whether the first part of the book is to be taken as a literal locust

plague or to be understood allegorically (that is,
figuratively of some future judgment). We must
decide for the literal view. An actual locust plague
had devastated the land. There are no hints in the
text itself that the prophet is using an allegory. The
picture given in the prophecy of the locusts is true
to their manner of action and to the results of their
blighting invasions: the disappearance of the vege-
tation in the fields; the eating of the bark of woody
plants together with the roots under the ground;
their swarms darkening the sun; their compact
march in military manner; the wind-like noise of
their movements; and the munching sounds accom-
panying their eating.

Was There Ever the Like?

The prophecy begins with a terse statement containing the fact of the divine revelation and the
recipient of it. One need only compare this super-
scription with that of Hosea or Isaiah in order to see
the difference in detail. For this reason we cannot
speak dogmatically as to the time of the ministry of
Joel. The prophet calls upon the old men especially
to recall whether they have known of any visitation
in their time or in that of their predecessors similar
to the locust plague which has devastated the land
by successive swarms of locusts. This judgment
could not be paralleled in the memory of any contemporary of the prophet. Because of the unheard of
character of the destruction the word concerning it is
to be passed on from generation to generation. Thus
is the unprecedented character of the calamity vividly
brought before us. It had never occurred on this

wise before. The four names in verse 4, meaning literally, the gnawer, the swarmer or multiplier, the licker, and the consumer or devourer, have been taken to mean either four types of locusts or four stages of growth in the case of one locust. (Note that the Authorized Version and the American Standard Version translate these Hebrew words alike.) Neither view is tenable, for the prophet uses the common word for locust ('arbeh) and then gives three poetic equivalents. What the prophet means to convey is this: in the successive swarms of the locusts what one portion of them left the other portion devoured. Notice the number four in the matter of judgments in Jeremiah 15:3 and Ezekiel 14:21. Some Hebrew commentators have tried to relate the four names to the four empires in Daniel 2 and 7. Nothing in the text warrants such allegorical treatment. Furthermore, we have only to compare Joel 1:3 with Exodus 10:2, 6, and Deuteronomy 28:38-42 to realize the literal import of the words of the prophecy. Locusts have rightly been called "the incarnation of hunger." They have been known to devour over an area of almost ninety miles every green herb and every blade of grass, so that the ground gave the appearance of having been scorched by fire. The locusts have a "scorched-earth policy" of their own. Joel's description of the plague has been confirmed by many accounts of locust devastations.

The Fearsome Plague

The drunkards are first called upon to awake out of the stupefying effect of their intoxication with wine. Compare Isaiah 5:11, 22, 23; 24:7-9; 28:7,

8; and Amos 6:1-6 for drunkenness in the land.
The drunkard, who is known for his song and
raucous laughter, is to weep, because his delightsome
vine has been destroyed by the locust plague. Note
the different mournings in this chapter: (1) the
drunkards, verse 5; (2) the nation under the figure
of a virgin, verse 8; (3) the priests, verse 9; (4) the
land, verse 10; and (5) the farmers and vinedress-
ers, verse 11. The locusts are now represented under
the figure of an invading nation, because of their
great numbers and the completeness of the desolat-
ing work. That the locusts are compared to a nation is no reason to infer that the plague was not a
literal one. See Proverbs 30:25-27 where ants are
pictured as a people along with locusts who are said
to have no king over them. The teeth of the locust
are likened to those of a lion and a lioness, because
the two jaws of the locust have saw-like teeth like the
eye teeth of the lion and lioness. Both the locust
and the lion are most destructive in their ravages.
Compare Revelation 9:7, 8. The extent of the
desolation is clear from the word concerning the vine,
the fig-tree, and all branches. The barks of the trees
were gone, and the branches were withered. And
all this desolation had been done to God's own land,
wherefore He calls them "my vine" and "my fig-
tree." .

Desolation Everywhere

The prophet thus far has noted in general terms
only the vast reach of the catastrophe. Now he fills
in the picture with well-chosen details. The accuracy
of the delineation is beyond question. God's people

Israel, under the figure of a young virgin who has
lost her bridegroom in death, are exhorted to lament
for the calamity that has come upon them. Why
this bitterest of all weeping? Because the offerings
of the house of the Lord (the meal-offering being
dependent upon the fruit of the field and the drink-
offering being dependent upon the produce of the
vine) were cut off. Even the worship of God's
house was affected by the desolation. What ravages
sin can introduce into every realm of life! No
greater catastrophe in the spiritual and religious
sphere could have overtaken them. This meant practically the setting aside of the covenant relationship
between God and His people. Mark you, we said
the setting aside of that relationship and not the
annulment of it. No wonder then that the priests
of the Lord gave themselves to mourning. Desolation touched everything: the field, the grain, the
vine, the olive tree, the wheat, the barley, the fig-
tree, the pomegranate-tree, the palm-tree, the apple-
tree, all the trees; in short, everything had under-
gone the blighting effect of the locust scourge. All
joy was gone because the harvest and vintage were
denied them. See Isaiah 9:4 and Psalm 4:7 for
the joy of the harvest and vintage. The gravity of
the situation is brought home to us by the accumulation of words describing ruin and desolation: "cut
off" in verse 9; "laid waste," "mourneth," "is destroyed," "dried up," and "languisheth" in verse 10;
"is perished" in verse 11; "withered," "languisheth,"
and "withered away" in verse 12. It was no unusual
locust plague about which Joel was writing.

Call to Fasting and Prayer

The Spirit of God through the prophet now instructs the people of God as to the way of return and blessing. Though the priests were mourning (v. 9) because of the interruption of the ceremonial life of the people, the Lord calls them to a girding with sackcloth, a wailing, and a lamenting that will bespeak their turning to the Lord with repentant hearts. The visitation of the locusts came not upon the land because the Lord delighted in judgment. Nay, He does not willingly afflict the children of men, but by chastisements, often severe but always purposeful, He would bring them back from their evil ways and from the pit of destruction. God is still the God of His people; note the use in verse 13 of "my God" and then "your God." The spiritual leaders of the nation are to proclaim and set aside a fast, convene a public gathering of all the inhabitants of the land, especially the elders who are to set the example, and then to cry mightily unto the Lord for His restoring grace. Since the judgment and calamity have been public, the humiliation and repentance must be also. God delights in prayer and heart piety and eagerly hearkens to the supplications of His people.

Token of the Day of Jehovah

Though the plague be literal and the prophet bewails the destruction wrought thereby, yet the plague in its literal sense does not exhaust the intent of the Lord. It points ahead to the coming great visitation of the day of Jehovah. This day is mentioned in 1:15; 2:1; 2:11; 2:31; and 3:14.

Because the day of Jehovah looms so large in prophetic Scriptures, we define it- and its relation to other days designated in the Word of God. In 1 Corinthians 4:3 Paul speaks of "man's day" (see American Standard Version margin). The day here spoken of is that in which we live, when man has sway and governs on the earth. To represent this rule God gave Nebuchadnezzar a dream of an image of a *man* (Daniel 2). This day will come to an end, as far as the Church is concerned, with the "day of Christ" which is the Rapture. See Philippians 1:6. After the Rapture "the day of Jehovah" begins. It comprises the time of the Great Tribulation on earth, the seventieth week of Daniel 9:27, and the time of the rule of the Messiah of Israel over them in Jerusalem on the Throne of David. See not only the Scriptures noted above in Joel, but Amos 5:18; Zephaniah 1:14-2:2 together with Isaiah 2:1-21 among many Scriptures throughout the prophetic books. At the termination of the day of Jehovah, the "day of God" will begin. In that day the elements will melt with fervent heat and the new heavens and new earth will result. This day lasts throughout eternity when God is all and in all. Compare 1 Corinthians 15:28. We have purposely elaborated upon these vital days, because the theme of the prophecy of Joel is The Day of Jehovah. With this truth in mind we can readily discern how the locust plague serves as a harbinger or foreshadowing of the coming day of Jehovah. Joel rightly views it with alarm. The then present judgment spoke clearly of the future terrifying day of judgment. The words "destruction" and "Almighty" are a play on

words (literally, "shod" and "Shaddai"). Not only
does the land suffer, but the beasts, the cattle, and
the flocks of sheep suffer as well. Animals suffer
with man, and especially so because of the drought
that attended the plague. The unrelieved drought
which affected the brooks and the pastures was as a
fire consuming what the locusts may not have
touched. The animals cannot pray so the prophet,
voicing his own desire toward the Lord in this crisis
and setting an example for all (v. 14), intercedes
for all.

What Is the Plague Now?

Words could not describe more vividly nor pun-
gently the distress made possible through a locust
plague. The chapter before us breathes heavily with
sorrow, mourning, wailing, and lamenting. Joy is
mentioned three times in the chapter (by three different Hebrew words), but only to say that it is cut
off from the people of Israel. Israel weeps again
today because of the overwhelming plagues upon her
from friend and foe alike. But, alas, a greater plague
than all grips the heart of the unbelieving Jew: it is
the plague of sin. Not trusting the Lord Jesus
Christ as Messiah and Saviour, the heart of every
Israelite is of necessity plagued with sin, weighed
down with many sorrows, and restless. Only Christ
can heal the plague, but so many of the patients do
not know the Great Physician. By the help of God
may we in these fast closing days be used to make it.
possible for many souls in Israel to be introduced to
their greatest need, the Physician of their sin-sick
souls, the Lord Jesus Christ!

QUESTIONS ON CHAPTER I

1. Indicate what is known of the personal life of the prophet Joel.

2. What difference in interpretation is found among students of this book?

3. How do you explain the events of the prophecy?

4. Describe fully the unprecedented plague which visited the land.

5. Point out the different groups in Chapter I which mourn because of the plague. Why is each so affected?

6. To what are the locusts compared and what are the results of their destructive work?

7. How was the worship of God's house affected by the locust scourge?

8. Does Joel show the way of return to the Lord and blessing? How is it to be accomplished?

9. Of what great prophetic period is the locust plague a token?

10. Define as clearly as possible the different days set forth in the Scriptures.

11. What is the nature of the great plague among Israel today?

12. How may it be remedied?

2

Chapter II

THE OUTPOURED SPIRIT

___

The Impending Day of Jehovah

JUST as the prophet Joel in the first chapter of the prophecy turned the minds of his contemporaries, who were filled with the sense of calamity because of the ruin wrought by the locust plague, from the visitation of the moment to a far worse judgment from the Lord, so he does throughout the second chapter of the book. There are men who have taken the position that the chapter deals solely with the locust plague; others maintain just as firmly that the passage is entirely future. Both views are extreme. As a matter of fact, Joel starts with the situation then existing in the land after the havoc of the locust plague, and then goes on to picture the dreadful Day of Jehovah yet future, but imminent.

"Sound An Alarm!"

It was the duty of the priests in Israel to blow the trumpets on specific occasions. See Numbers 10: 1, 2, 9. The Lord is here calling upon them to blow the trumpet of alarm from God's holy mountain, from the place of His sanctuary and the center of their worship. Why? What was the threatening calamity? The Day of Jehovah was at hand. Here we have an elaboration of the prediction in 1:15. The locust visitation was a clear indication of what

events were yet in store for Israel in the imminent
Day of Jehovah. Why this day, this time of judgment, is so terror-inspiring is now set forth by Joel.
It is a day of darkness, gloominess, and thick clouds.
Darkness is a figure in Scripture for misery and distress. Note in this connection such passages as
Isaiah 8:22; 60:2; Jeremiah 13:16; Amos 5:
18ff.; and Zephaniah 1:15, 16. The figure is a
most telling one because locust swarms by their
density do obscure the light of the sun. Some students of the passage have found it difficult to take
the words "as the dawn spread upon the mountains"
to refer to the darkness just mentioned, because of
the evident contrast between light and darkness. For
this reason it has been suggested that the comparison
with the dawn be taken with the following words
concerning the great and strong people. But this
explanation is not wholly necessary. The points
of comparison are these: just as the dawn is sudden
and widespread, so will the darkness of the Day of
Jehovah be. What great and strong people the
prophet is alluding to can be discerned from the latter part of the verse where it is clearly stated that
there never has been the like nor will there be in
the future. We have proof here that an ordinary,
or even extraordinary plague of locusts is not the
final and ultimate fulfillment of this prophecy. The
Spirit of God through the prophet is pointing to an
unparalleled foe of the people of God who will in a
coming day inflict greater desolation than did the
locust plague. Who is this enemy? With many other
students of the book we understand it to be the
Assyrian power of the future, the northern power

of the last days. Study carefully Isaiah chapter ten
and Daniel chapter eleven.

Destruction on the March

The record now paints for us an eye-witness account of what ruin the drought and the locusts
accomplished in the land. The drought was as a
consuming fire that leaves all scorched in its trail,
and with the locusts what was as the garden of
Eden before they descended upon the land, was now
nothing more than a desolate wilderness. Nothing
escapes the devastating blight. Now follows an ac-
curate description of locusts in their march, an account unexcelled in all the realm of literature. The
locusts are likened first of all to horses; in fact,
the head of the locust is so like that of a horse that
the Italians call it *cavalette* (little horse) and the
Germans speak of locusts as *Heupferde* (hay horses).
They not only look like horses but they have the
speed of the war-horse. Compare Job 39: 20. And
noise accompanies all their movements, noise as when
chariots jostle in their running, noise as when fire
licks up the dried stubble, noise as when a strong
host is being mustered for the conflict.

The noise of the wings of the locusts in motion
and of their hind legs strikes terror in every heart.
In the life of every member of the nation this visitation will long linger in memory. The locusts are as
tireless in their running as mighty men of war; they
appear to have their regulated phalanxes like an army
on the march (see Proverbs 30: 27) ; they are adept
at scaling walls; as though directed by a master
mind, they do not break their ranks; no one

thrusts another out of his place. All is in turmoil
and in confusion at their onslaught. The heavenly
bodies themselves are darkened by the thick masses of
locusts flying under the whole expanse of the heavens.
Destruction is literally on the march, for as thieves
the locusts· seek out what they may devour. But
the Lord Himself is in all this as well. He utters
His voice—the thunderstorm—before His great army
of locusts. They are His army in a real sense because they are both powerful and numerous. One
of the laws of Mohammed reads: "Ye shall not
kill the locusts, for they are ·the army of God
Almighty." The command of God is being executed
by His instruments.

   If this be so terrible that man can scarce abide it,
how much less will he be able to do so in the hour
when God's fullest judgments will be upon a Christ-
rejecting and God-dishonoring world, in the Day of
Jehovah? Here we find one of the great principles
of God's dealing with man throughout his history:
God only inflicts punishment after great provocation,
and when He does so, it is meant to draw man back
from further and more severe visitations of the
wrath of God. The plague of locusts was severe,
but it could not approximate the devastation to be
wrought in that time known as the Day of Jehovah.
Says God: "From the lesser learn the greater and
be warned."

The Call to Repent

   What grace God offers them! Even at that late
hour it was possible to repent and turn to the Lord,
thus averting further disaster. God calls for a time

of deep exercise of heart and spirit, a time of fasting, a time of brokenness of heart before Him. Because it is ever so easy to substitute the external for the real, to be lost in the round of outward show, God exhorts them to rend their hearts and not their garments.

The rending of garments on occasions of great mourning is recorded early in the Scriptures (see Genesis 37:29, 34; also 1 Samuel 4:12; 1 Kings 21:27; and Isaiah 37:2). It was meant to convey that broken and rent condition of the heart of the mourner. Because the sign often replaces the reality, God through the prophet enjoins a true and genuine contrition of heart. All such action before God is based upon the fact of God's wonderful character, for He is gracious beyond words and ready to forgive. God is always more willing to bless than to blast, to pardon than to punish, to win by love than to wound by lashing. So there is always the possibility of God's displeasure being turned into His favor, when His people come low before Him. God has no delight in the death of the wicked, but that he turn from the evil of his ways and live. Note the case of the Ninevites in Jonah 3:9. Upon true repentance God will restore to them plentiful harvests. The meal-offering and the drink-offering, both dependent upon the harvest of the field and vineyard, had ceased because of the drought and the plague, but will now be available to repentant Israel. See 1:9, 13, 16.

"Call a Solemn Assembly"

Again the priests are called upon to blow the trumpet in Zion. The first trumpet (compare verse

1 of this chapter and Numbers 10:5) was to sound the alarm to warn of the threat of an invading foe; the second trumpet (verse 15 of this chapter and Numbers 10:10) was for the purpose of a convocation in Israel to gather the people to the sanctuary of the Lord. To this assembly all are to come, old men, infants, children, even the bridegroom and the bride who ordinarily are exempt from all public obligation (Deuteronomy 20:7; 24:5). All are guilty, so all must humble themselves before God. Personal, individual joys are to give way to the interests of the entire community. The priests, the ministers of God, are to assume their rightful places of responsibility and lead the people in their penitent crying unto the Lord. The very words are indicated which are to be spoken: "Spare thy people, O Jehovah, and give not thy heritage to reproach, that the nations should rule over them." Can you conceive of the blessing with which these words are fraught? How such attitude of heart lays bare the mighty arm of God on behalf of His people. Would that the Church of the living God were aroused throughout its length and breadth to pray that such turning to God may be realized in our day among the dry bones of the house of Israel. The very ends of the earth would feel the impact of such a turning of Israel to God. In apostolic days it was simply stated that men from among Israel with the message of God turned the world upside down; flaming evangelists from among Israel today can have no less of the power of God at their disposal now. All too long have the nations of the earth trodden Israel under foot with seeming impunity. Because God has not

rent the heavens and come down visibly on their behalf, the hearts of 'God-defying nations have been hardened to continue their domination of Israel and to cry, "Where is their God?" But the hour of God's prophetic clock cannot be far off when Israel shall turn in penitence to the living God from whom they have grievously strayed, and God will requite the nations in their bosom fully for the havoc they have wrought upon the heritage of the Lord and the woundings they have perpetrated upon the apple of His eye. Then they will know the answer of their ridicule of the omnipotent God as though He were helpless to aid His own and as though He were unmindful of the covenant relationship which He has brought into being between Himself and Israel.

The Answer of God

When the faintest cry of the penitent is uttered, it does not escape the ear of the Lord. His zeal and His jealousy on behalf of His people are aroused and He goes forth to bless them unstintingly. He remembers the wounds of His land and He heals them. He is mindful of the sorrows of His people and He graciously solaces them. The grain, the new wine, and the oil, long withheld because of their sin, will be restored; the land will give its produce and they will be abundantly satisfied. God will remove their reproach among the nations, and He will exalt them as head of the nations. In that conclusion of the day of Jehovah the Lord will utterly rout the army of the invading Assyrian, the army of the northern power. (Literal locusts, mark you, would scarcely be called "the northern army.") The land

barren and desolate is Arabia, the eastern sea is the
Dead Sea, and the western sea is the Mediterranean.
In short, the army will be divided and completely
annihilated. All this will come upon the enemy because he has exalted himself in his pride. See the
Book of Nahum concerning the pride of the Assyrian,
also Zechariah 10: 11.

Rejoicing and Restoration

The Assyrian enemy may attempt great things, but
the Lord will truly accomplish great things for His
people. That land and people which languished,
mourned, and wept shall have its sorrow turned to
joy. First of all, the land is told to rejoice and be
glad (verse 21). Its desolate condition was vividly
portrayed in the first chapter (see verses 17 and 19).
Then the beasts of the field are called upon to put
away their fears, for now there will be pasture and
the fruit of the tree and vine. Formerly they had
panted for lack of water and food (compare 1: 18-
20). Finally, in the climaxing word the children of
Zion are to rejoice in the Lord (note 1: 16). First
there will be temporal blessings and then additional
spiritual blessings. God will give them the former
and latter rain in due and proper measure, that
amount necessary where the drought had prevailed.
It is of great interest to the student of the Word of
God to know that the rains have increased in Palestine within recent years, but the grand fulfillment is
yet future when Israel turns to the Lord. Once the
rains are no longer withheld there will be plentiful
harvests of wheat, wine, and oil. Yea, the very losses
sustained through the locust plague will be restored

and more.   The years that the locusts have eaten will
be forgotten in the new bounties.   The locust plague
did not last for years, but one such devastation could
have results for years.   The locusts were God's great
army which He personally had sent.   There will be
the enjoyment of God's bounty now that Israel is
reconciled to her God, and she will be satisfied.   God
will be praised by His people and they shall never
suffer shame again.   They shall never be put to
shame.   Verses 26 and 27 end with the same words
because God would give fullest assurance of the
truth stated.   In verse 26 it is used of temporal benefits; here it is of spiritual benefits.   God is the sole
and only necessary guarantee that all these will be
accomplished.

Never Put to Shame

God in the midst of Israel in blessing: is not this
the goal of all His dealings with them?   And what
provision He has made for this very thing in the
gift of His Son to be their Messiah and Saviour from
sin.   How can we stand idly by without letting them
know of this Saviour and Lord?   How can they hear
without a preacher?   How can God receive His rightful praise from redeemed hearts in Israel except
they hear and believe the message of the Gospel of
Christ?   In all this plan God has a place, a real
place, for you and me.   May we be quick to see it
and ready to obey.

The Outpouring of the Spirit

Verses 28 through 32 form chapter 3 in the Hebrew text; and chapter 3 in the English translations

is chapter 4 in the original. No one will be inclined
to doubt that the disclosure of truth in 2:28-32 is of
sufficient importance to warrant its appearing in a
separate chapter. Sad to say, this vital passage (with
its New Testament counterpart in Acts 2:17 ff.)
has been grossly misunderstood and made to teach
what was never intended. The first safeguard is to
note the time indicated in the passage. The events
set forth here are placed chronologically in that time
designated as "afterward." What does that time
mean? We find it in Hosea 3:5 and there it is
coupled with "in the latter days." The prophet is
speaking of the latter days for Israel, a period which
covers both the Tribulation period and the reign of
the Messiah which follows it. Compare carefully
Isaiah 2:2, and Peter's words in Acts 2:17. Our
passage cannot be fulfilled until Israel is returned to
their own land. At that time God will pour out His
Spirit, the blessed Holy Spirit, upon all flesh. Several truths are implied here: (1) the figure employed is taken from the analogy of the rain (see
2:23); (2) the pouring out reveals the Spirit is
from above; and (3) the Spirit is given in abundance. The outpouring of the Spirit is to be upon
all flesh. It will be universal in character and scope.
But does this mean universal for all Israel or for all
mankind generally? Expositors of the passage are
divided, some holding to one position and others
holding to the other position just as positively. No
one, however, will deny, from the context and the
prophetic teaching of other portions of the Old Testament, that all Israel surely is included. Differ-
ences of age (young and old), sex (sons and daugh-

ters), or position (servants and handmaids) will constitute no barrier nor hindrance to this gift of the Spirit. There is no recorded case in the Old Testament where the gift of prophecy was granted to a slave. In the latter days, however, the fond desire of Moses (Numbers 11:29) will be realized. The dreams, visions, and prophecy spoken of here are the three modes mentioned in Numbers 12:6. Note that verse 29 reiterates the same truth given in verse 28: "I will pour out my Spirit." The time element is also repeated. We must not think that this is the first mention of an outpouring of the Spirit of God upon Israel in the Old Testament prophetic books. See Isaiah 32:15; 44:3, 4; Ezekiel 36:27, 28; 37:14; 39:29; and Zechariah 12:10. But that day will mean wrath and judgment upon the unbelieving. God will perform mighty transformations both in heaven and on earth. The sun and the moon will be affected; blood and fire (as in Exodus 7:17 and 9:24) and pillars of smoke (as in Exodus 19:18) will be visible. It will be the great and fearful day of Jehovah. Nevertheless, the outpouring of the Spirit will result in salvation. There will be those who call upon the Lord unto physical deliverance and whom the Lord will call unto spiritual salvation. Notice the two-fold use of the thought of calling: (1) calling on God (this means salvation, see Romans 10:13) and (2) God calling them. God has foretold that there would be an escaped remnant (compare Obadiah 17 as well as Zechariah 14:1-5) and these will be a blessing to the whole earth. What large dividends the world will reap for the labors expended by the people of God to give Israel the gospel! No

human mind can comprehend the increase. Sufficient
it is to nerve our every endeavour and quicken our
flagging zeal on behalf of the lost sheep of the house
of Israel.

The Fulfillment of the Prophecy

At this point it is in place to ask whether Joel's
prophecy has been fulfilled in Acts 2. At the outset
it must be made clear that it is incorrect to say there
is no connection between the two passages. Peter
distinctly states that he is referring to the prediction
of Joel. However, that fact alone does not constitute
a fulfillment. In the first place, the customary formula for a fulfilled prophecy is entirely lacking in
Acts 2: 16. And even more telling is the fact that
much of Joel's prophecy, even as quoted in Acts 2:
19-20, was not fulfilled at that time. We cannot take
the position that only a portion of the prophecy was
meant to be fulfilled at all, because this would work
havoc with Bible prophecy. God predicts and He
can perform just what He predicted. The best position to take is that Peter used Joel's prophecy as
an illustration of what was transpiring in his day
and not as a fulfillment of this prediction. In short,
Peter saw in the events of his day an earnest that
God would yet completely bring to pass all that Joel
prophesied. Joel's prophecy, then, was prefilled; it
is yet (as the Old Testament passages on the outpouring of the Spirit show) to be fulfilled.

QUESTIONS ON CHAPTER II

1. How does Joel treat the locust plague in this
chapter?

2. Why is the trumpet of alarm to be blown by the priests?

3. Show how the plague of locusts exactly conforms to the coming judgment of the Day of Jehovah.

4. Who will be the enemy of God's people Israel in the future Day of Jehovah? Give proof from Scripture.

5. Why are the locusts likened to horses?

6. How are they similar to an army on the march?

7. What is God's offer of grace in that hour of distress?

8. How does the trumpet call of verse 15 differ from that of verse 1?

9. To whom does the call to assemble pertain? Why?

10. What would be the result if the Church of our God were to cry out to the Lord on behalf of lost Israel?

11. How will God yet answer the cries of the godless nations in their persecution of Israel?

12. Indicate the manner in which God answers the penitent cry of Israel.

13. What will be the result of the invasion of the Assyrian forces in the Day of Jehovah?

14. Describe the blessings of restoration set forth by Joel. What temporal and spiritual blessings are promised?

15. What is the goal of all God's dealings with Israel? How can we have a part in this?

16. What is the time indicated in the prophecy in 2: 28-32?

17. Outline the outstanding details of the prediction.

18. What other Old Testament Scriptures speak of a future outpouring of the Holy Spirit upon Israel?

19. What will be the portion of the unbelieving at that time?

20. How will Israel's turning to the Lord in faith affect the condition of the nations of the earth?

21. Has the prophecy of Joel 2:28-32 been fulfilled in Acts 2? Give proof for your answer.

Chapter III

THE JUDGMENT OF ALL NATIONS

NO PROPHET of the Old Testament has a more important revelation of the end times than the one now before us in the third chapter. How gracious of God to let us know the exact time of these happenings. They will take place when the Lord Himself returns the captivity of Judah and Jerusalem. The return of Israel to the land will never be fully accomplished until the Lord does it by His omnipotent power. Note Jeremiah 23:1-8. At the time of God's regathering of Israel to the land He will gather all nations into the Valley of Jehoshaphat to judgment. The prophet evidently has in mind the historical narrative in 2 Chronicles 20. Tradition has assigned the judgment to the Kidron Valley; though this tradition is only from Eusebius' time (fourth century A. D. on), there are those who believe it to be correct. The site indicated must be in or near Jerusalem. The method of God's gathering of the nations to the judgment is set forth in verses 9-12 of this chapter. Compare also Zechariah 12:1-3, 9; 14:2-4; Isaiah 29:1-8. One of the most important features of the judgment is the basis of it: the nations will be judged for God's people and for His heritage Israel. Read carefully Matthew 25:31-46 and note the words "my brethren." The same judgment is in view in both passages. Without doubt our Lord Jesus Christ had this passage in mind when He concluded His marvelous Olivet Discourse.

The great sin of the nations—all will be involved in
it in the time of Jacob's trouble (Jeremiah 30:7)—
is that against Israel. Little do the nations realize
how they incur the wrath of God when they lay vio-
lent hands upon His heritage and the plant of His
choosing. He will not suffer it always. Joel shows
the day of reckoning has come because Israel was
scattered among the nations; their land was divided;*
they were sold to indulge the vilest passions—a night
of revelry or debauchery. Josephus, the historian,
tells us *(The Wars of the Jews,* Book VI, chap. 9,
paragraph 2; also his *Antiquities,* Book XII, Chap.
7, par. 3; and I Maccabees 3:41; II Maccabees
8:11, 25) that in the Roman wars the enemy chose
out of the Jews "the tallest and most beautiful, and
reserved them for the triumph; and as for the rest
of the multitude that were above seventeen years old,
he put them into bonds; and sent them to the Egyptian mines . . . those that were under seventeen
years of age were sold for slaves." Such indignities
and worse have been perpetrated upon God's people
in our own day, and the end is not yet. Will God

---

* Author's note: Since these lines were penned, the United
Nations' Committee on Palestine has made its investigation
and submitted its report with its recommendations. The
minority report advocated a bi-national federal union in the
Holy Land; the majority opinion favored the partition of
Palestine into Arab and Jewish states. The latter opinion
was adopted by the United Nations in session at Lake Suc-
cess, New York, on November 29, 1947, the plan to be
implemented in 1948. It will be readily seen how momen-
tous was this decision, for the nations have already gone on
record as advocating the partition of the land, for which
God foretold through Joel that He would bring all nations
into judgment. We await with great expectancy the out-
working of this plan. Another word of our God has been
fulfilled: "they parted my land."

visit with judgment for these? Verily, verily He
will.

Divine Retribution

The Lord through His prophet now addresses
Tyre and Sidon as representative of all the land of
Phoenicia. Do they think they can fare differently
from all the rest? Do they not realize that they in-
jure God in the person of His people? All the
grievances committed upon God's people, He con-
siders as done to Himself. If men think they can
strike at God, He will show them that swiftly and
speedily divine retribution will overtake and over-
whelm them. God will not keep His silence for ever.
The prophet recalls the plundering of Judah and
Jerusalem by the Philistines and the Arabians in the
time of Jehoram (2 Chronicles 21:16, 17). The
very ones sold afar off will God use to bring about
His judgment upon His and their foes. Instead of
the children of Judah being sold for sport or profit,
the sons and daughters of their enemies will be sold
into the hand of the people of Israel who in turn will
sell the enemy into the hand of a nation afar off. The
fate which they planned for Israel will rebound upon
the head of Israel's godless adversaries.

The Armies Mustered

God calls upon the nations to prepare for war;
this is the method whereby He brings the nations to
their deserved judgment. The word "prepare" is
literally "sanctify"; that is, by sacrifices and appropriate rites and ceremonies. See 1 Samuel 7:8, 9
and Jeremiah 6:4. This is to be war to the finish.
To that end let all the nations muster and mobilize

their manpower to the very hilt. Let them come
fully equipped and accoutered. In order that no man
lack proper weapons let every tool used for peaceful
pursuits, the plowshares and the pruning-hooks, be
beaten into swords and spears. (Who of us will
soon forget the preview of this in World War II
when we had our "scrap drives"?) So great will be
the desire to destroy God's people that even the weak
will fancy himself to be strong. What an assemblage
that will be! The nations will be banded together
and confederate as never before (see Psalm 2:1-3).
In the midst of the scene which passes before the
prophet's vision he prays that God's mighty ones
(His hosts) may come down, in contradistinction to
the supposed "mighty ones" of verse 9. Now the
whole theme is summarized for us in verse 12. The
nations are seen as bestirring themselves to the white
heat of wrath against Israel; their objective is the
Valley of Jehoshaphat (how appropriately is it thus
named: "Jehovah judges"); and there they (the
nations) will meet the blessed King of Israel, their
Protector through all ages, and their Champion in
their darkest and blackest hour, the Lord Jesus
Christ, who will sit ready to judge once and for all
the accumulated sins of the nations against Israel.
Fearful day that will be, and the nations will as
easily escape it as they can cause the sun to cease
shining in the heavens. Just as the Lord speaks to
the nations in verse 12, so He commands His agents
of judgment. The judgment is described under the
double figure of the harvest and the vintage. The
harvest is ripe and the winepress and vats are full to
overflowing. What this means is stated in literal

language: "for their wickedness is great." This
judgment is referred to in Isaiah 63:1 ff. and promi-
nently in Revelation 14:14-20. Terrific will be the
impact when God's mighty ones meet the mighty
ones of the nations in mortal and final combat. The
issue will not hang in doubt; it is all clearly stated
beforehand. The life-blood of the nations will drench
the soil of the earth. How unspeakably sad that the
nations will not learn the lesson regarding God's
people, the Jews, before it is too late! Oh, Lord,
open Thou the eyes of many of them to see aright
and their ears to hear aright! Remember that this
is not a caprice with God, for the wickedness of the
nations is insufferably great.

"Multitudes in the Valley of Decision"

But the story is so ponderous that it must be told
out further. The prophet sees the nations assembled
in innumerable hosts in the valley where God (not
they) will make His decision. The repetition of the
word "multitudes" is meant to show how innumerable they are. As far as the eye can possibly see, the
hosts of the peoples of the earth are drawn up in
array—a great sea of surging humanity. The valley
of decision defines more clearly the Valley of Jehoshaphat. There the words of decision: "Come,
ye blessed of my Father" and "Depart, ye cursed"
(learn here the literalness of the words of Genesis
12:1-3), will be uttered with the voice of the mighty
Son of God, voice as the sound of many waters.
Heaven and earth will feel the force of this judgment, and the Lord Himself will be roused up as a
lion. Indeed, the Lion of the tribe of Judah will

utter His voice from Zion and Jerusalem. Creation
will resound at the voice of Him who in that hour
will be the refuge of His people (blessed King of
Israel that He is) and a stronghold to the children
of Israel. The Lord will dwell in Zion and all will
be holiness for God's people. Compare Psalm 132:
13, 14. No strangers will pass through her any
more to plunder, to destroy, or to pollute. When
they do come, it will be to worship the Lord of hosts.
Zechariah 8:20-23.

Blessings on Judah

The judgment on the nations, however, is never
meant to be an end in itself. Through it God means
to bring blessing to His people Israel. Joel concludes now with words of promise for God's down-
trodden ones. Even the mountains and hills (ordinarily the least productive of all soil) will flourish
abundantly. Water will be present in great supply;
a perennial fountain will furnish all the water needed.
The Valley of Shittim, on the border between Moab
and Israel beyond Jordan, known for its dryness,
will be well-watered. Egypt and Edom, representative of all Israel's enemies (that such is the case can
be readily seen from the "all" of verses 2, 11 and 12),
will be made a desolation forever. But Judah and
Jerusalem shall abide eternally. God's people will
remain, and by judging the nations the Lord will
wipe away the blood-guiltiness of the nations in their
persecution of God's people. Note verses 19, 21.

How Far Away?

As we meditate on this marvelous disclosure in
God's Word, we are driven to the question, How far

off can it be? Not very far, beloved in Christ. Then evangelize Israel!

QUESTIONS ON CHAPTER III

1. In what prophetic hour do the events of chapter three take place?

2. Where will the judgment of the nations be set?

3. What is the basis or ground of the judgment? Present New Testament proof.

4. How extensive will this judgment be?

5. What are the specific charges against the nations?

6. Does the partition of the land in our day fulfill Joel's prophecy?

7. What is God's grievance against Tyre and Sidon?

8. How are the armies of earth mustered for the final and fatal conflict?

9. Who brings them low in battle? What figures are used to describe the catastrophe?

10. What other prophetic passages speak of this same judgment?

11. Of what struggle do verses 14 to 17 speak?

12. How does the prophet picture the people of Israel in prosperity and blessing?

13. Of whom are Egypt and Edom representative? Give proof.

14. In view of the nearness of the time of these events, what should our attitude be toward Israel?

AMOS:
THE RIGHTEOUSNESS OF GOD

Chapter I

ORACLES AGAINST THE NATIONS

The Messenger of God

AMOS, whose name occurs nowhere else in the
Old Testament outside of his prophecy, was
born in the southern kingdom of Judah in Tekoa.
He was not the son of a prophet (see 7:14, 15) nor
a prophet from his birth (compare Jeremiah 1:5),
but was a herdsman, a sheep-tender, and a cultivator
of sycamore trees. He was not of a family of rank,
wealth, or influence, but given to the pastoral life in
the rugged regions of Tekoa. His figures and images,
beautiful and abundant, are drawn from rustic life.
His book is characterized by beauty of expression
and loftiness of thought. He was a contemporary of
Hosea and, although born in Judah, was sent by God
to prophesy to the northern kingdom of Israel at
Bethel, its religious center. While Hosea emphasizes
the love of God in the midst of His judgments, Amos
sets forth the majesty and uncompromising righteousness of God against sinners. His prophetic messages
and visions are (with the exception of the last) of
a threatening nature. They are directed against the
low moral condition of the people and especially

against their apostasy from the Lord to the worship
of idols.

The Time of His Ministry

The days of Uzziah in Judah and Jeroboam II in
Israel were marked by great prosperity, in fact, the
most prosperous for the northern kingdom. Israel
was at the height of its power under this king. The
period was one of great wealth, luxury, arrogance,
carnal security, oppression of the poor, moral decay,
and formal worship. The moral declension and spiritual degradation of the people were appalling. Amos
foretold chastisement from the Lord, but did not
name the foreign invader—Assyria—the scourge of
the Lord. Though verse one of this prophecy men-
tions Uzziah, it is clear that the object of the
prophecy is Israel in particular. Tekoa, the home
of the prophet, was twelve miles southeast of Jerusalem and six miles south of Bethlehem. The time of
the message is dated as two years before the earthquake. Earthquakes are not uncommon in Palestine,
but this must have been of unusual severity for it is
mentioned more than two centuries after this by
Zechariah (14: 4, 5). Josephus the historian claims
the earthquake took place when Uzziah tried to assume priestly functions (2 Chronicles 26: 16-23),
but this is without proof and useless for the purpose
of dating the event. We have no means of ascer-
taining the time of this terrifying visitation in nature,
a warning in itself of the judgment yet to overtake
them.

Roaring from Zion

Amos relates his message immediately to that of
Joel by declaring that the Lord will roar as a lion

from Zion (compare Joel 3:16). The roaring of
the Lord is here against Israel; in Joel it is for
Israel against her enemies. When the lion roars, he
leaps on the prey. Judgment is about to fall upon
Israel. The pastures of the shepherds in the south
and the top of Carmel in the north are mentioned as
comprising the whole land in this stroke of judgment.
Carmel is the great promontory on the Mediterranean Sea, rich in pastures, oliveyards, and vineyards. See Isaiah 35:2. If Carmel withers, how
great will be the desolation elsewhere? The withering is not of drought alone, but destruction in general is meant.

Judgment on Syria

The prophets Isaiah, Jeremiah, and Ezekiel also
have prophecies against foreign nations, but they
place such oracles after the indictments against God's
own people Israel. Amos reverses the order and we
shall see the wisdom of the arrangement in due
course. Judgment will fall first upon Damascus,
the capital city of Syria. The nations chosen, representative of a larger number as we know from other
prophetic passages, are those noted for their oppression of Israel. Those are mentioned last as a sort
of climax (Edom, Ammon, Moab) who were related
to Israel. The expression, "for three transgression
. . . yea, for four," which occurs with each an-
nouncement of punishment (giving an intended im-
pression of uniformity) does not have in mind a
mathematical enumeration. These nations are being
visited not for three or even four transgressions, but
for an incalculable number. The expression means

the measure of iniquity is full and wrath must fall
upon the wicked. The punishment cannot be turned
away: it is inevitable; it is irrevocable. How had the
Syrians filled up the measure of their iniquities
against God's people, Israel? They had threshed
Gilead with iron threshing instruments. Gilead was
the territory east of the Jordan belonging to the
tribes of Reuben, Gad, and the half tribe of Manas-
seh, a region especially open to attack from Syria on
the north. The atrocity mentioned here—the tear-
ing and mangling of bodies with iron threshing
sledges—was perpetrated by the Syrian king, Hazael
of Damascus, in his oppression of Israel under Jehu
and Jehoahaz. Note 2 Kings 10:32, 33; 13:3-7.
How ancient are these diabolical deeds and yet how
reminiscent of the dastardly acts so recently committed upon God's people Israel. The prophets of
Scripture are the inspired commentators on the historical events of the Word of God. In each case the
punishment is set forth as fire, that of war and
destruction. See Jeremiah 49:27. Hazael and Ben-
hadad were two of the most grievous oppressors of
Israel. The Ben-hadad referred to may possibly be
both Syrians of that name, but probably the son of
Hazael (II Kings 13:3) is meant rather than the
Ben-hadad who was slain by Hazael (II Kings 8:
7, 15). Breaking the bar meant the breaking of the
gate of the city and the consequent entrance of the
besieging enemy. The Valley of Aven is probably
the present day Bekaa, between Lebanon and Anti-
libanus, of which Heliopolis (Baalbek) was the most
important city. Beth Eden is a district near Haran,
and Kir is an Assyrian province on the banks of the

river of the same name. The judgment predicted here came through the Assyrian Tiglath-pileser who drove the Syrians to Kir. II Kings 16:9. Thus Syria was to be visited for her cruelties to Israel, and especially would the blow fall upon Damascus, that renowned city of which the Arabs have said: "If there is a garden of Eden on earth, it is Damascus; and if in Heaven, Damascus is like it on earth."

Doom of Philistia

Gaza stands in this chapter as representing all Philistia, as is clear from the mention of Ashdod, Ashkelon, and Ekron in verse 8. Gath is omitted from the mention of the cities of the Philistine Pentapolis probably because it had already been destroyed by King Uzziah (2 Chronicles 26:6). The sin of the Philistines was that they took an entire captivity, leaving no one, and delivered them up to Edom, probably Israel's most inveterate enemy. Wholesale expatriation of an entire region, and not the exiling of a few war captives, is meant. Some understand it was for commercial purposes. If we compare this passage with Joel 3:3ff. we shall see that the matter was accomplished after this manner: the Philistines sold a portion of prisoners to the Edomites and the remainder to the Phoenicians who in turn sold them to the Greeks. Then, as now, it seemed highly profitable to the enemies of Israel to make merchandise of the people of God. What historical events are alluded to here? It has been suggested that these cruelties took place in the reign of King Ahaz when the Philistines invaded the cities of the lowland and the south of Judah. See II Chronicles 28:18. It is

more probable that the prophet is referring to the
invasion of Judah by the Philistines in the reign of
Jehoram. II Chronicles 21 : 16. Decimation of the
population of Philistia will be the answer of God for
these misdeeds. Turning His hand against Ekron
speaks of His visiting them again with the same
judgment.

Wrath Upon Phoenicia

The prophecy against Tyre is meant for all Phoenicia. The crime in this instance is the same as that
of the Philistines—the selling of prisoners of war as
slaves. The Phoenicians were known as a great
commercial people and must have disposed of the
prisoners of war to more than one nation. The
prisoners may have been taken in the course of the
wars of Israel with Hazael and Ben-hadad of Syria,
from whom the Phoenicians could have obtained
them. These transactions were all the more grievous
when perpetrated by the Tyrians, because there had
been a brotherly covenant of long standing between
King Hiram of Tyre and David and Solomon. Note
carefully II Samuel 5 : 11; I Kings 5 : 2-6, 15-18;
9 : 11-14. Moreover, no king of Israel or Judah ever
made war upon Phoenicia. The judgment announced
in verse 10 was made good when parts of Tyre were
burned with missiles of the Chaldeans under Nebuchadnezzar.

Punishment for Ammon

The Ammonites, also related to Israel, had at-
tacked Jabesh-gilead under Nahash. Compare I Samuel 11 : 1. They also joined the Chaldeans in their
invasion of Judah for plunder. II Kings 24 : 2. But

the atrocities touched upon in verse 13 are not mentioned in the Old Testament historical accounts. They were carried out for the purpose of expansion. It is the new but ever old cry of extermination for expansion, for "Lebensraum" as the Germans call it. The tables will be turned and Ammon will be the object of the foreign invader. Rabbah (Deuteronomy 3:11), the capital city, called by the Greeks Philadelphia after Ptolemy Philadelphus of Egypt and now known as Amman, will be visited by invasion and captivity. See Jeremiah 49:3. What a refutation is a chapter like this to the contention 'that Israel's God was considered a tribal or national God. He is Lord of all the earth as the Scriptures maintain throughout.

Hands Off Israel!

This chapter speaks with divine eloquence of the danger involved in touching Israel, the apple of God's eye, for harm. God has not only reproved kings for their sakes (Psalm 105:14) but nations as well, as this portion of His Word so amply attests. Is it not patent that the Word of God contains its own authentication of the promise of God that He would curse him that cursed the seed of Abraham? What a commentary is this chapter, with many others which could be added here, on the faithfulness of God to carry out every word He has ever uttered. Remember also, dear reader, that the other portion of the promise is still true as well: God blesses those who bless Abraham's seed. Know you of a greater blessing on earth in this day which could be theirs, comparable to having the gospel of their Messiah, the Lord Jesus Christ, preached to them?

We have practically reached to the uttermost part
of the earth in our missionary endeavours; when,
oh when, will we ever get to Israel dying without the
Saviour, the only Hope of Israel? By God's grace
let us bestir ourselves that the gospel may be heard
in Jerusalem, among the natural children of Abraham. In this path lies unspeakable blessing, for God
has so solemnly promised.

QUESTIONS ON CHAPTER I

1. Outline briefly the personal history of Amos.

2. What is the burden of his message to Israel?

3. Describe the days in which he ministered.
Against whom was his message particularly directed?

4. What figure is used of God in judgment and
what is it intended to convey?

5. How does Amos differ from Isaiah or Jeremiah
in his oracles against foreign nations?

6. Upon what nation does judgment first fall?
What is the reason for this visitation?

7. What is meant by the expression "for three
transgressions . . . yea, for four"?

8. What historical events are referred to in verse
3? Give Scripture references.

9. What judgment is foretold for these sins and
through whom was it carried out?

10. What is the sin of the Philistine cities?

11. To what historical events is allusion made
here?

12. What punishment is foretold by Amos?

13. What was the crime of Tyre and when was it
perpetrated?

14. Why was the sin of Tyre all the more grievous?

15. How was the prediction of judgment carried out?

16. Why was Ammon to be visited with God's punishment?

17. What stroke of God's hand is threatened them?

18. What unforgettable lesson is to be gleaned from this chapter?

19. How is this chapter a commentary on Genesis 12: 1-3?

20. What constitutes the greatest blessing that the child of God today can offer a lost Israel?

Chapter II

THE SINS OF ISRAEL

Indignation Against Moab

THE second chapter of Amos' prophecy carries on the word of condemnation against the nations which was begun in the first chapter. The indignation of God is now stated to be against Moab. The climaxing sin of this nation was the burning of the bones of the king of Edom into lime. Vengeance was poured out even upon the dead. It reveals a spirit of revenge which will not stop even at death. This incident is not recorded in the historical books of the Old Testament. It has been suggested, and it is probable, that it took place at the time of the war between Jehoram of Israel and Jehoshaphat of Judah, with the king of Edom, against the Moabites. See II Kings 3:26, 27. For such a display of unrestrained wrath God will visit Moab with the fire of destruction. Kerioth, one of the prominent cities of Moab, will find her palaces consumed by fire. Compare Isaiah 15:1; Jeremiah 48:24, 41, 45. The death of Moab with tumult, shouting, and the sound of the trumpet, as well as the cutting off of the judge and princes, was realized when Nebuchadnezzar completely subjugated Moab; from that time it no longer existed as a nation.

Sins of Judah

The nations are punished for sins against the laws of nature, conscience, and natural feeling; Judah

and Israel are visited because they sinned against the
revealed will of God. Note the important truths set
forth in Romans 2: 12, 14, 15. Verses 4 and 5 of
this chapter are directed against Judah, while the
remainder of the Book of Amos is addressed to
Israel. God is not partial, so even His people, when
guilty, must be judged. The cycle of prophecies was
meant to end with the people of God. They had
what the heathen nations never had—the law of the
Lord in the commandments of Moses. But they paid
no heed to it and cast it from them, failing utterly
to keep the righteous statutes given therein. They
engaged themselves with lies, their false idols, which
led them farther astray from the way of God's
choice. Note Psa. 40: 4 and Jer. 16: 19, 20. Bad
example has a way of perpetuating itself, so we find
that the fathers of Amos' contemporaries also followed in their day the same worthless idols. Pre-
ceding generations were guilty of the same sins. The
judgment pronounced in each case is that of fire—
1: 4, 7, 10, 12, 14; 2: 2, 5. The palaces of Jerusalem were devoured by fire when the hosts of Nebuchadnezzar captured the city in 586 B. C.

Transgressions of Israel

The iniquities of Israel are now set forth in all
their heinous details. God cannot gloss over the
failures and sins of Israel, if they are to realize the
gravity of their spiritual decline and turn in true
penitence to the Lord from whom they have so
grievously revolted. The Scriptures tell us that he
who oppresses or mocks the poor, reproaches His
Maker (Prov. 14: 31; 17: 5), and God surely

4

espouses the cause of His poor and righteous ones.
In Israel, because of the insatiable greed of unrighteous judges, the one who had a righteous cause was
condemned by the judge for the sake of a bribe.
This violated the clear prohibition of the law in
Deuteronomy 16:19 and other passages. For the
paltriest sum, even a pair of shoes, the tribunals of
that day could be bought (see also 8:6). The sin
of despising the poor is mentioned several times in
this prophetic book: 2:6, 7; 4:1; 5:11; and
8:6. The ungodly are further said to pant after
the dust of the earth on the head of the poor. What
does this mean? Various have been the explanations
of this part of the verse. It has been suggested that
the prophet is saying that the wicked bring the
poor so low by oppression that the latter cast dust
on their heads in mourning. For this custom in
mourning, widespread throughout the East, note 2
Samuel 1:2 and Job 2:12 among others. Another
view is that the ungodly tread the poor in the dust
of the earth under their feet. Still others think the
creditors begrudged the poor even the dust which
they, as mourners, cast on their heads. Probably the
first position is the best; that is, the unrighteous
cannot rest until they have brought the poor down to
the very depths of sorrow. And because the meek
are not forward in presenting and maintaining their
just case, they are taken advantage of and their cause
is perverted. Compare Isaiah 10:2. Their greed is
accompanied by unbridled lust. Father and son go
to the same maiden, probably one of the prostitutes
attached to idol temples, such as that of the goddess
Astarte. Invariably spiritual departure from the

Lord is followed by moral departure as well. The
result is, whether by intent or not, that the holy
name of the Lord is profaned. God is disgraced in
the vile actions of His people. See II Samuel 12:14.
As children of God in this wicked world we are
exhorted of God, since we have named the name of
Christ, to depart from iniquity. II Timothy 2:19.
We either grace the grace that saved us or we dis-
grace the grace that saved us. But Amos has not
concluded his indictment of the guilty ones in the
northern kingdom of Israel. He appears to have
left the worst for last as a kind of climax. The
wicked were laying themselves down beside every
altar upon clothes taken in pledge. The outer garment is meant. Exodus 22:25-27 and Deuteronomy
24:12, 13 commanded that this be returned before
sunset, so that the poor could have it as his covering
for the cool night. They not only refuse to return
the garment but lie on it themselves, and that in idol
temples (I so understand the words "every altar,"
for this could hardly refer to the central temple of
God in Palestine). The dastardly character of this
sin (or rather several sins compounded) grows on
one the more it is contemplated. When those who
know the light commit sin, they often go to greater
extremes than those who know not God at all. Light
rejected ever results in greater night. The wine
which these revelers drink in their idolatrous and
obscene feasts to their god (not "God") has been
bought with the money which they procured through
unjust fines. Oppression was rampant and they were
speeding on to judgment at the hands of an infinitely
righteous and holy God.

God's Former Mercies

To bring out by marked contrast their base ingratitude to the Lord, Amos enumerates some of the gracious benefits which Israel has received at the hand of the Lord. The benefits of God to Israel are in themselves accusations against the nation for their sins. Rebellious though they were, the Lord had destroyed the Amorite (Joshua 24:8) before them. The Amorites were the most powerful of all the nations inhabiting the land of Canaan, and in this verse they probably stand representatively for all. Note how this nation is singled out repeatedly in Genesis 15:16; 48:22; Deuteronomy 1:20; Joshua 7:7. The description given of them is vivid—tall as the cedars and strong as the oaks—and shows that the report of the unbelieving spies was right as far as outward appearances were concerned. See Numbers 13:22, 32, 33. Their trouble was that they reckoned not on the power of God, as did faithful Caleb and Joshua. Though the enemies were giants in stature God destroyed both their fruits and their roots, in a word, utterly. For the same figure compare Ezekiel 17:9 and Malachi 4:1. Moreover, the destruction of the enemy in the land had been preceded by the favour of God in liberating the nation from Egyptian slavery and in preserving them for forty years through the wilderness wastes. Psalm 44:3. To climax all these bounties, God raised up of their sons, when dwelling in the land, those who were to bear the message of His will to the nation, the prophets, and He gave of their young men to be Nazirites. See Numbers 6. God had done all to

provide for their instruction in the truth and in
His will and for the maintenance of purity and holiness of life in the nation. Though the vow of the
Nazirite was of one's free will, yet it is said that
God raised them up because the desire and impulse
to such action came from Him. In these men, young
men at that, God gave Israel extraordinary examples
of purity of life and complete dedication to the Lord.
Now the prophet turns and asks in point-blank manner: "Is it not even thus?" "Will you dare to
deny or dispute this?" Did Israel delight in these
mercies of God and render the Lord grateful service? The Word of God gives the devastating answer:
they tempted the Nàzirite to breach of his holy vow
and to unfaithfulness and sought to silence the message of the prophet of God. Compare 7: 12-14 (Amos
experienced this very thing in his own ministry) and
Jeremiah 11: 21. Could brazenness and defiance ex-
tend further? No. So Amos foretells the hour of
their visitation.

Inescapable Judgment

The opinion has been given that verses 13 to 15
tell of a destructive earthquake. The visitation is to
be war as is clear from the actions pictured in the
remaining verses of the chapter. Not all verses in
either the Old or New Testaments are as easy of
translation as they appear in our versions. Does
verse 13 in the original speak of Israel being pressed
under the Lord as a cart is pressed that is full of
sheaves? Or is it the Lord who is pressed under
them in that manner? (See the American Standard
Version margin for the latter.) Surely it is the first

view, for the second would give an inelegant picture
of the Lord, to say the least. The thought of the
verse is that Israel has been running the gamut of
sin in departing from the Lord; she has owned and
obeyed no check or restraint to her wayward life.
Now God will press her down in her place; He will
hem her way in so that she will not be able to escape.
The swift, the strong, and the mighty will be helpless before the judgment of the Lord. Flight, force,
and deliverance will fail these men in the hour of
need. The trained bowman, the foot soldier, and
the horseman (all these indicate, incidentally, that
the scourge is that of war) will find their prowess
unavailing in this calamity. Even the bravest among
the mighty will be able to save only his life. In
short, none will escape the Assyrian army when they
come to carry out God's purposes of judgment upon
His sinful people. The rod of God's anger will fall
and no one will be able to evade it in that fearful
day.

"Is It Not Even Thus?"

If the prophecies of Amos thus far reveal anything,
they show clearly that their central message is this:
there is no turning back of the judgment of God after
His repeated offers of grace and blessing are spurned
or refused. And this is true today. It is rightly
called the day and age of grace, for the evident reason that God is offering graciously eternal life and
glory to those in Israel and throughout the world
who will trust the Lord Jesus Christ for their salvation. Apart from God's offer there is only the hope-
less doom of perdition. But how can men accept
that which has not been plainly presented to them?

There are many of Israel in this Gospel-enlightened land of ours who have not heard the story of redeeming love in their Messiah and Saviour, the Lord Jesus Christ. And many more in other lands, perishing and languishing for the crime of having been born Jews, who know nothing of God's plan of redemption. We must get the message to them, because the Lord has entrusted it to us. Is it not even thus?

QUESTIONS ON CHAPTER II

1. What condemnation does the prophet speak forth against Moab?

2. What is the probable time of the occurrence of these events?

3. How was the judgment of God carried out in accordance with this prophecy?

4. What difference can be seen between the sins of the nations and those of Judah and Israel?

5. Why does the cycle of threatening prophecies conclude with the people of God?

6. Wherein had the people of Israel sinned?

7. How was the prediction of the prophet fulfilled in the life of the southern kingdom of Judah?

8. From 2:6 to the end of the book what portion of the nation is continually in view in the prophet's words?

9. Describe the transgressions of the judges in Israel.

10. What are the various interpretations of 2:7? Which is the most probable to you and why?

11. How did sins of a spiritual character lead to sins of a moral nature?

12. Define clearly why the sins mentioned in verse 8 were of such a grievous type.

13. How does Amos bring out the base ingratitude of Israel toward the Lord?

14. What mercies of the Lord are given prominence here?

15. How did Israel react to the bounties of the Lord?

16. What are the possible explanations of verse 13? Which do you prefer? Why?

17. How extensive will the destruction be?

18. What is the central message of the prophecies of Amos?

19. Is there any hope for Israel today apart from God's offer of grace in the Lord Jesus Christ?

20. What, then, is our duty toward Israel now? Are we performing it?

Chapter III

PRIVILEGE AND RESPONSIBILITY

God's Choice of Israel

AMOS directs his prophecies primarily, but not exclusively, to Israel, the northern kingdom, as did the prophet Hosea. The third chapter begins with the call, "Hear this word." For the same expression see 4:1; 5:1; also note 3:13. All Israel, the whole family that God brought up from Egypt, is addressed, though Ephraim is especially in view. What is the message of surpassing importance that both parts of the nation must hear? God says that of all the families of the earth (note the contrast with "family" of verse 1) He has known only His people Israel. To know them in the sense of this passage is to choose them, to set them apart for His own purposes. God took them to be His people and accorded them special privileges for testimony. Read carefully such passages as Psalm 1:6; 144:3; and John 10:14 for this meaning of "know." For the special choice of Israel see such passages as Exodus 19:5; Deuteronomy 4:20; 7:6; Psalm 147:19, 20. We may have expected the prophet to declare that, because God has chosen Israel, He will overlook their failures and sins. The unknowing and the unbelieving often accuse God of such partial dealings with His people Israel, as though He could deny His holy character no matter who is involved. The Word of God states the opposite of man's inferences: be-

cause God has taken Israel into a place of intimacy
with Himself, He will all the more assuredly visit
upon their heads all their iniquities. Nowhere in the
.Bible is a more vital and basic principle enunciated.
The prophet is saying that punishment is commen-
surate with privilege. Of the one to whom much is
given, much is expected. Judgment must begin at
the house of God (I Peter 4: 17). The nearer we are
to the Lord in relationship, the more is faithfulness
required of us. We cannot and dare not plead that,
because the world about us cares not for the missionary passion of the Lord Jesus for Jew and Gentile
the world over, we need not arouse ourselves to carry
the Gospel to them. Even the laxness of other be-
lievers can never be our standard. The prophet
thunders against his people that the choice of God
was never meant as a cloak for wickedness. Because
God had chosen the Church in New Testament times
to be His channel of blessing through this age of
grace, did not preclude His visiting wickedness with
judgment when it manifested itself. See the case
of Ananias and Sapphira in Acts 5: 1-11. The angels
of heaven who sinned against the greatest light have
no redemption provided for them at all. II Peter
2: 4 and Jude 6. Great is the blessing of nearness
to God, but great also is the responsibility of living
in conformity with such light.

Judgment Follows Sin

In verses 3 to 8 the prophet establishes his right
to announce the judgment of God on his contemporaries. The aim of this series of seven questions is
to show the people the relation between the prophet's

utterances and the events of the day. In the natural world, the realm of nature, nothing happens by accident or chance; so in the sphere of God's dealings there is always a cause for every effect. The first question is: Can two people walk together except they appoint a specified time and place, agreeable to both? When we see two walking together, it is taken for granted that they have had a previous arrangement and are of like mind. The former fact is the effect, while the latter is the cause. Transferred into the realm of Israel's spiritual condition, God asks how He can walk with Israel and look in favour upon them when they are walking in sin. At one time God walked with them (Jeremiah 3:14) because they were agreed, but now the ways of Israel and the way of the Lord are so diverse that there can be no fellowship between them. Compare II Corinthians 6:16, 17; James 4:4. If the Lord seems afar off, dear reader, may it not be that you have left off walking with Him? Do the things He puts first loom largest in your life? After personal holiness and purity of life, do you desire earnestly that the Gospel shall be given to the lost? And what of Israel in the plan of God to reach the unsaved? When we walk close by the side of the Lord Jesus, we shall find ourselves oft praying for Israel and visiting the lost sheep of the house of Israel. The second question is: Does a lion roar in the forest when he has caught nothing? Amos knew well the habits of the lion and understood the lion's roar to mean that the prey had been caught. In like manner God only threatens (Joel 3:16; Amos 1:2) when He is preparing to punish. The same thought

is expressed by a different figure in Matthew 24:28.
A related question is: Will the young lion (who
remains in his lair) cry out of his den, if the old
lion has taken nothing? As a matter of fact, when
the old lion approaches with the prey, the young
lion is aroused. The underlying truth is that, if
Israel's sins did not merit and call forth judgment,
the prophet would not be crying out against them.
The threatening predictions of the prophet are the
effect, while the cause is the sinful state of the
nation. The next question is just as pointed: Will
a snare spring up from the ground where it has
been placed without something having been caught
in it? So the instruments of God's judgment will
find their object, because they have gone in the way
of their sin. The first clause in verse 5 states the
same question as the latter part but from a slightly
different viewpoint. The answer is exactly the same
in both instances, and in both cases the prophet still
has sinning Israel in mind. A hint that the trumpet
of war will yet be blown in the land is given in the
following question: Will the trumpet be blown in a
city and the people not be afraid? The nation was
well acquainted with the trumpet for festal gather-
ings (Numbers 10:2, 7; Joel 2:15) as well as that
for warfare (Numbers 10:9; Joel 2:1). And who
was it that would not be filled with fear and forebod-
ings when the alarm for war was sounded? Who
among Israel should not fear now when Amos is
sounding the alarm of the approach of God's swift
instruments of visitation? The last question in the
series has suffered much from misinterpretations. It

has been made to teach that God is the cause of evil,
that is, moral evil. Such a position runs counter to
all the teachings of the Scriptures. Note James 1:
13, 17. The query is: Does evil befall a city without
the hand of the Lord being in it? The difficulty
has arisen (as in so many other cases) because of a
failure to recognize that the word "evil" has more
than one meaning depending upon its use. Here it
does not mean moral evil, but calamity. Study carefully Genesis 19:19; 44:34; Exodus 32:14; Isaiah
45:7; and Ezekiel 7:5. In short, God is the One
who brings your trials and calamities upon you for
your sins. The secrets of His dealings He reveals
to His servants the prophets; thus they can speak
forth the mind and purpose of God. God warned
Noah of the flood; He told Abraham of the destruction of Sodom and Gomorrah (mark Genesis 18:17
with John 15:15); He forewarned Joseph of the
seven years of famine; and so with His servants
down through the centuries of Israel's history. Even
our Lord Jesus warned the apostles of the coming
desolation of Jerusalem (Luke 21:20-24). Just
as surely as there is fear when the lion roars, then,
there must be prophesying when the Lord Jehovah
speaks. The prophet cannot but prophesy. He must
obey God no matter how the people react to his message. Amos prophesied, as did all the prophets of
God, because he was impelled by divine constraint
to do it. What surer authority did the prophet need?
None, because he had the authority for his message
from the omnipotent God Himself.

Oppressions of Samaria

The Lord now addresses Himself to His prophets that they may spread this word upon the palaces of Ashdod and of Egypt. It was not only customary in the East to assemble on the flat roofs of the houses, but from that vantage point, especially the highest roofs of the palaces, the invitation could go out broadcast through all the land. The nations are bidden to come together upon the mountains of Samaria to behold what tumults and oppressions are to be found in that city. Ashdod stands here as representative for all of Philistia. Samaria was built on one mountain (I Kings 16:24), but there were other mountains surrounding the city. From these mountains surrounding Samaria, men could see what was transpiring within the city. If these pagan nations steeped in idolatry condemn Israel, then how much more the righteous God? The great tumults were occasioned by the oppression of the poor. See Isaiah 5:7 for the same truth. The sad part of it all is that the people no longer know to do right; sin has blinded their ability to discern. Jeremiah 4:22. It was so long since they had done good, that they were out of practice. Sin's blinding power is only too real, as all know who have been enlightened by the Spirit of God. The palaces of Samaria were full of those things gained by violence and robbery. Note Proverbs 10:2. The punishment is now stated in abrupt and vivid language: "An enemy, round about the land." The abruptness of the text brings out the idea of suddenness and presents the threat in bolder relief. Those very palaces which stored up plunder (see verse 10) will in turn be plundered. Men's sins carry with them their own dire punishments. The fulfillment of all this warning is found in II Kings 17: 5. Yet in wrath God remembers mercy, so He rescues from the destruction a small remnant—likened here to two legs or a piece of an ear—of all that are living in ease in Samaria. The picture is that of a shepherd trying to save from the devouring lion even the most insignificant parts of the sheep, because of the shepherd's love for his own sheep. Only such a small part will remain of those who are living in extravagance and luxury (note also 6: 1, 4) in the capital city. The corner of the couch or the divan is the most comfortable and is the place of honor. The mention of silken cushions, made of costly stuffs, adds to the picture of careless self-indulgence. (There is the possibility of reading the last part of verse 12 as "and in Damascus on a bed." The reason is that the same letters are employed in the original to spell "damask" or the material, or the city of Damascus. The name of the city would then be parallel in thought to Samaria. But how did the people of the northern tribes get to Damascus? It is suggested that at the time of the Assyrian invasion the city was in the power of the Israelites, already conquered by Jeroboam II, as stated in II Kings 14: 28. After the city had been taken by the northern kingdom, probably many residents of the northern tribes went there to live.)

The Day of Visitation

The same ones as in verse 9 are called upon to testify against the house of Jacob, all twelve tribes. Mark the accumulation of names for God in order to

bring out the solemnity of the declaration and the
assurance of its fulfillment. The altars of Bethel,
which were supposed to be a refuge for them, would
be the first to suffer from God's visitation. The
golden calves are here in view. See I Kings 12:32;
13:2. Amos, like Hosea, traces all their calamity
to their departure into idolatry. With idolatry cut
off their own personal home life will also be destroyed. The winter-houses and the summer-houses
(of the nobility and rich as well as of the royalty)
together with many houses will be brought to a sad
end. Homes, sumptuously decorated with walls,
doors, and ceilings of inlaid ivory, will suffer the same
fate as the rest. For Ahab's house of ivory see
I Kings 22:39; also Psalm 45:8. Prosperity abused
and misused can only issue in utter and irreparable
loss.

What About the Remnant?

In the midst of this sad recital of privilege abused
and of light rejected there is sounded the glorious
note of God's love which must have a remnant, no
matter how small, though all the rest be destroyed.
And the Scriptures are clear that now God has in
mind a remnant from among His people Israel.
Romans 11:5. This remnant can only be called out
of Israel through the preaching to them of the Gospel
of the Lord Jesus Christ, their Messiah and Saviour.
Will we make it possible? The King's business re-
quireth haste, and may God give us all diligence in
the task.

QUESTIONS ON CHAPTER III

1. Who are addressed at the beginning of this
chapter?

2. Did God ever choose Israel from among the nations of the earth?   Give Scripture proof for your answer.

3. What is the specific meaning of "know" in verse 2?

4. What great truth concerning privilege and responsibility is found in this passage?

5. Does this principle apply to God's missionary program among Jew and Gentile?

6. What is the purpose of the series of questions in verses 3 to 8?

7. Explain the thought of the prophet in this portion.

8. Apply each question to the condition of Israel in Amos' time.

9. Can it be maintained on the basis of verse 6 that God is the cause of moral evil or sin?   Defend your answer.

10. To whom does the Lord reveal His secrets? Illustrate.

11. What is the purpose of the gathering of the nations to the mountains of Samaria?

12. What was the condition of the people within the city of Samaria?

13. Indicate the predicted judgment and its fulfillment.

14. What is the meaning of verse 12?

15. Why are the names of God accumulated in verse 13?

16. Where will the judgment strike and why?

17. In what way does the love of God appear in the midst of this chapter on God's visitation?

18. Relate Romans 11: 5 to the prediction of Amos in this particular.

5

Chapter IV

PREPARE, O ISRAEL!

"Ye Kine of Bashan"

THE fourth chapter of Amos' prophecy begins with the same call to hear which we met in the previous chapter. The address is now directed to the kine of Bashan. Bashan is that territory east of the Jordan River between Mount Hermon and the mountains of Gilead. The kine of Bashan were noted for their well-fed and strong condition, for the pastures of this region were lush. Compare Deuteronomy 32:14; Psalm 22:12; and Ezekiel 39:18. There are some students of this passage who think, although feminine forms of expression are used here, that the nobles of Samaria are meant by the prophet. They hold that the feminine is employed only to show the effeminacy of the aristocracy of the land. We prefer to see, with many others, the luxury-loving and extravagant women of the capital of Samaria in this reference. Such a usage is not contrary to prophetic Scriptures. See Isaiah's denunciation of the wanton women of Zion in Isaiah 3:16-26, as well as 32:9-13. That land is not far from the judgment of God whose womanhood is degraded, and such was Samaria in the days of our prophet. In order to enjoy their luxuries these women oppressed and crushed the poor. The form of expression used shows this was their habitual action. Their lords, that is, their husbands (Genesis 18:12), they con-

tinually urged to provide them with the needs for
their drunken revelries and debaucheries. Mark how
oppression and idolatry (see verse 4) go hand in
hand. Because of such contempt for the will of
God and because of the profanation of His name,
He swore by His holiness (for He can swear by no
greater) that they would be carried off into exile.
This deportation is given under the figure of a fish-
erman catching fish with fish-hooks. They will be
helpless and completely at the mercy of their cap-
tors. Captives were led by their conquerors by a
hook through the nose. See II Kings 19:28 and
II Chronicles 33:11 (note the margin of the American Standard Version for this verse); also Jeremiah
16:16; Ezekiel 29:4; and Habakkuk 1:15. The
résidue mentioned in this passage refers to what is
left over from the taking away with hooks, not the
posterity of the prophet's contemporaries. In the
siege of the city the women, driven on as though
cattle, will go out at the breaches of the city walls,
broken open by the enemy. Each one will go straight
before her, not allowed by the enemy to turn to
either side and rushing headlong to escape the terror
and death in the city. The latter part of verse 3 is
admittedly very obscure. The difficulty arises from
the fact that a word is used (the Hebrew "hahar-
monah") which occurs nowhere else in the Old Testament. This accounts for the numerous and varied
views presented for the explanation of the passage.
Suggested translations are "the Rimmon image,"
"Hadadrimmon," "the mountains of Armenia," "the
mountains of Monah," or "palace." With so little
evidence upon which to proceed and with such variety

of opinions, we do well to avoid dogmatism on this
point.   Probably what is meant is that in order to
facilitate their flight from the enemy they will cast
themselves into a certain land or district which they
hope will afford them the necessary refuge for the
hour.   More than this we cannot say, except to add
that most recent Biblical atlases know nothing of a
site called Harmon.   The thought of the prophet,
however, is quite clear: exile will be the portion of
the   pleasure-loving,   poor-oppressing,   unfeeling
women of Samaria.

Misdirected Zeal

Amos turns now from solemn declaration to biting
and bitter irony.   He invites the whole of the kingdom, not merely the women, to come to Bethel and
transgress and to frequent Gilgal and multiply transgression.   On the very surface it is evident that the
words are ironical, because nowhere in the Bible
does God reveal Himself as countenancing sin or
inviting to it.   Bethel and Gilgal are specifically mentioned because of the manner in which they had perverted the places of most sacred memories to the
nation.   See Genesis 35:1ff. and Joshua 5:1-9.
Verses 4 and 5 give a true picture of the way in
which the people adhered to their idol practices and
yet were careful in keeping certain appointments or-
dained by the law of Moses.   They were bringing
their sacrifices every morning as the law had commanded.   Numbers 28:3, 4.   They were adhering
to the letter, while transgressing it by their calf-
worship.   God is here giving them up to their own
idolatrous worship.   They were also paying their

tithes every three years (not every three days as
the American Standard Version suggests), conform-
ing in this also to the regulations of the law. Compare
Deuteronomy 14:28; 26:12. There are those who
understand the next exhortation to offer a sacrifice
of thanksgiving of that which is leavened as contrary
to the precepts of the Mosaic law. A study of the
Levitical regulations will show that frankincense was
laid on the meal offering (Leviticus 2:1, 2, 8), as
commanded here, and that leavened bread was commanded to be offered with the sacrifice of thanksgiving (Leviticus 7:12, 13). Thus far all that has been
stated shows they were unusually meticulous in the
carrying out of the details of the laws for worship.
True, their proclamation and publishing of freewill
offerings (see Matthew 6:2) savors of self-will in
their worship, for he states definitely that such
pleased them. They were intent on ultimately pleas-
ing themselves instead of God (so in Zechariah 7:
5, 6). But the emphasis is scarcely on these short-
comings. The words are meant to convey that everything was outwardly in order and done according to
law, yet in the doing of them they were multiplying
transgression. Why? Because at the same time they
were steeped in all the debasing forms of idol worship. God is not pleased with the divided heart, with
the limping between two opinions. He is the only
God and brooks no rival in worship. Thus, though
they were going through the rounds of worship, they
were sinning because their hearts were not wholly
unto the Lord. See Ezekiel 20:39 and Matthew
23:32.

God's Judgments Unheeded

Since their gifts to God were so displeasing to Him, He gives them chastisements in return. The list of chastisements recorded in verses 6 to 11 reveals not only the obstinacy and sinfulness of Israel, but the unremitting and exhaustless love of God. It is a love that will not let the loved one go. And the punishments were all intended to prevent greater chastisements. Yet at the end of each visitation it is stated that they had not returned to the Lord in spite of all His dealings. Note the repetition of "yet have ye not returned unto me, saith Jehovah" in verses 6, 8, 9, 10, 11. We are reminded in this recital of Isaiah 9:13; Jeremiah 5:3; and Hosea 7:10. The repetition by Amos marks the persistent opposition, bringing out forcefully their stubbornness and impenitence. The first calamity was famine which is described vividly as cleanness of teeth and want of bread. God had taken away the material necessities of life to bring them to their senses and to set aright the spiritualities of life. There is no need to seek for a historical confirmation of this in the historical books of the Old Testament, because God did this more than once. One example is to be found in II Kings 8:1. Though they hungered, yet they sought not the Lord in repentance and faith. The second visitation was drought. God withheld rain three months before the time of harvest. This is disastrous. Reference is made to the latter rain of the spring which is so vital for the development of the corn and the grain for a bountiful harvest. But the withholding was not universal: it rained on one city and not upon another. This was purposeful to show that the giving or withholding was not by chance, but by the sovereign act and choice of God. Scarcity of water compelled the inhabitants of the cities visited by drought to go long distances for the necessary water to carry on life. Another stroke of judgment was the blasting and mildew, the very judgments predicted in Deuteronomy 28: 22 for disobedience to the law of God. Blasting is the effect of the withering east wind from the dry desert. Note Genesis 41: 6. In the mildew (from excessive drought, not moisture) the ears became yellow without grain. To climax this a locust plague devoured vineyards, fig trees, and olive trees (compare Deuteronomy 28: 39, 40, 42). Life was surely being made unbearable from the physical standpoint alone, but the impenitent heart stores up for itself wrath unto the day of judgment. See Revelation 16: 21 for the effect of the judgments of the Great Tribulation upon defiant hearts. The sad refrain continues that they did not for all this return to the Lord. Like Pharaoh of old they steeled their hearts the harder against the wooings of God. Next, the plague after the manner of Egypt, where it was native, was sent upon them. Deuteronomy 28: 27, 60. And the choice of the manhood of the nation was slain in prolonged and recurring warfare; their boasted cavalry was carried away into exile. So great was the number of the slain on the battlefields that their unburied corpses filled the air with stench. Surely they would turn to the Lord by this time, but the record states that they continued in their obdurate disobedience to the Lord. Lastly, Amos recalls that they underwent

overturnings and desolations comparable only to
God's overthrow of the wicked cities of Sodom and
Gomorrah. Some think reference is made to the
earthquake of 1:1, but the information at hand is
insufficient to decide definitely. Probably what is
meant is a summary of all the previous visitations.
Compare Isaiah 1:9. So trying were the inflictions
of the Lord's hand that the people narrowly escaped
complete destruction. See Zechariah 3:2 and I Corinthians 2:15. For the fifth and last time Amos
notes that even so the people were not minded to
return to the Lord. What a picture is before us,
dear reader, of the obstinate heart of man which will
not lightly turn to the Lord, nor, indeed, after many
chastisements! May we ask God earnestly to deliver
us from such a heart of unbelief and wickedness.

The Coming Calamity

Now the prophet is prepared to declare to Israel
the consequences of such opposition to the Lord and
His will. Because all the previous chastisements did
not produce in them the fruits of repentance and
faith, God says, "Thus will I do unto thee, O Israel."
But the prophet never states what the punishment is
to be! The undefined character and uncertainty con-
nected with the coming calamity make the fear and
apprehension all the greater. Since they did not
heed God's providential warnings, they must now
meet Him face to face. It will not be indirectly by
way of His judgments, but directly, person to person.
Some interpreters understand this warning to mean
that they are to prepare to encounter God as their
enemy and not for the purpose of reconciliation.

Although this is surely a possible meaning, a probable explanation is that the prophet is holding out to them the last and final warning. They had better get ready to meet God Himself, not His judgments, and give Him an answer for their impenitence. Who this God is that they are to meet is set forth in majestic terms. He is the omnipotent Creator, forming the mountains and creating the wind; He is the omniscient God who knows every thought of man; He is the ruler over all nature who can turn the morning light in due course into darkness; and He, the mighty Lord God of hosts, is the sovereign over all the places of the earth. The five participles of the original bring out the majesty of God as constantly operative in His created universe of matter and man. This is the Mighty God whom Israel must be ready to meet!

Prepare, O Israel!

The very exhortation of the prophet to Israel to prepare themselves to meet God tells forth its own unspeakable urgency. The matter will not permit of delay; it cannot be avoided. How much more urgent is it this hour. May we help Israel to hear and live!

QUESTIONS ON CHAPTER IV

1. Of whom is Amos speaking in the phrase "kine of Bashan"? Explain.

2. What were their sins against which the prophet prophesies?

3. How does Amos picture the deportation of the guilty ones?

4. To what interpretation do you come concerning the latter part of verse 3?

5. What is the meaning of the prophet's irony in verses 4 and 5?

6. Wherein lay the inconsistency in the actions of the people?

7. What was the ultimate intent of all Israel's worship?

8. How did God try to bring His people back to Himself? Did His judgments have the desired effect?

9. What clause shows the continued obstinacy of Israel in their sins?

10. Enumerate and discuss the different visitations on the people.

11. Does judgment always lead to penitence? Illustrate from Scripture.

12. What is God's final answer to the unbelief and waywardness of Israel?

13. Was Israel prepared then to meet God face to face?

14. Is she any better prepared now for such a meeting?

15. What would God have you do about it?

Chapter V

EXHORTATION TO REPENTANCE

Dirge Over Israel

THERE is a note of finality about the conclusion of the fourth chapter which would cause one to believe that all was over for Israel. But this chapter shows that in the midst of warnings God in His infinite love holds out the brightest promises for obedience and faith. The fifth chapter begins with a lamentation over the ruin of Israel. Amos views the northern kingdom as though the stroke of judgment from God had already overtaken the ungodly. The ruin is complete. The virgin Israel is fallen with no prospect of recovery; there is no one to whom she can look to aid her in her present plight. She is addressed as virgin, not because of the beauty of the land nor because of her hitherto unconquered condition (see Isaiah 23: 12), but because this is customary prophetic usage in personifying countries or states. Note Isaiah 47: 1. We must beware that we do not misinterpret the word concerning Israel's rising no more. The statement has its emphasis in relation to the exile of Israel and not for the indefinite future ages, because this would deny the restoration of Israel (mark carefully Isaiah 27: 6), a glorious return of God's people abundantly attested in all the prophetic writings, as well in the New Testament as in the Old. The invasion of the Assyrian will be costly in human life; only a tenth

will be spared. This prophecy and others throughout Amos and the other prophetic books of the Old
Testament show how literally God meant the warnings of Deuteronomy 28. Compare Deuteronomy
28:62 with verse 3 of this chapter. We have described for us, then, the utterly prostrate and helpless condition to which the northern kingdom was to
be reduced by the Assyrian foe.

Exhortation to Seek the Lord

Before the judgment falls there is still an opportunity for repentance and restoration. God is loathe
to close the door of grace and mercy. In Noah's day
He waited (Genesis 6:3; I Peter 3:20) one hun-
dred and twenty years before He shut the door
(Genesis 7:16). Let us not be impatient with the
patience of God if He tarries for the lost among
Israel that they too may be saved to make up the
Body of Christ with us. The prophet's words are
short (two words in the original) but freighted with
blessing for those who would hear. The exhortation
to seek recurs in verse 5 (in the negative), 6, and
14. Again and again the love of God calls His wayward ones. It is the Lord they must seek and not
the places of idolatrous worship—Bethel, Gilgal, and
Beersheba. The first two cities have been before us
in the previous chapter (v. 4) to which are added
Beersheba, hallowed by memories of the past (especially Abraham, Genesis 21:33) but now a place
to which pilgrimages were made for the worship of
idols. See 8:14 of this prophecy. Since this town
was about 25 miles south of Hebron, one can get an
inkling of the territory that had to be covered to

reach this spot.   Amos testifies that to seek after these idol shrines is to pursue that which is to come to nought.   Again the call is repeated to seek the Lord and live; otherwise, the Lord would break forth as fire (we saw how often this was the judgment in the first chapters of this book) upon the house of Joseph.   God is likened to fire in Isaiah 10:17; Lamentations 2:3; and Hebrews 12:29. The house of Joseph is a less frequent name for the ten tribes whose most important tribe was Ephraim, the son of Joseph.   Obadiah 18; Zechariah 10:6. Of the many guilty ones in the kingdom the unrighteous judges are singled out, for they have turned justice into wormwood (6:12), that which is bitterly wrong.   Justice is sweet, but injustice is bitter, obnoxious, and injurious.   By their acts they have cast righteousness to the ground.   Now, in contrast to their unjust ways they are reminded to consider Him, the righteous Judge, who is also the omnipotent Lord.   He is altogether sovereign in nature: the Pleiades and Orion (well known constellations appearing in Job 9:9; 38:31) are the work of His hands;   He brings about the changes from day to night and vice versa; the floods (with a possible allusion to the flood of Noah's day) are in His control.   He also can bring sudden and irreparable destruction upon ungodly men and their carnal reliances.   It is Jehovah with whom they have to do:

The Evil Time in Samaria

The unjust judges of Samaria have grievously sinned against the Lord, for they are denounced once more.   In the gate, the public place of assembly where tribunals were held, they hated such as reproved their ungodly ways and despised any one who spoke uprightly. The poor were trampled under foot and had to pay for justice if they were to obtain it. They used taxes from the poor (possibly they took interest too which was forbidden) on themselves, instead of returning it to the needy who could ill afford to pay it. As a result they, the judges, were able to have homes of hewn stone which were costly dwellings (Isaiah 9:10), for houses were usually made of sun-dried bricks. But ill-gotten gain is never enjoyed and short-lived at the best. They would not dwell in their fine homes, and would not enjoy the fruit of the vineyards they had planted. See Deuteronomy 28:30, 39. In the time of Israel's glorious restoration the reverse will be true. Isaiah 65:21, 22. The transgressions and sins of the unrighteous and bribed judges are called manifold and mighty. How God hates unjust judges! The times were so evil that it seemed the better part of prudence to keep silent concerning these outrages. Those who were wise spiritually knew that protests under such conditions could only make matters worse.

Entreaty to Repentance

Yet again Amos beseeches them to seek good and not evil, so that they might live. Then would God be with them indeed, and not as they were falsely comforting themselves on the presence of God with them. Their claim was empty pretense based on the fact that outwardly they continued in the worship of the Lord. They are counselled to hate evil, love good, and do justice, so that the Lord may display

His grace to the remnant of Joseph. Although
Hazael and Benhadad had wrought great havoc in
the northern kingdom (II Kings 10:32, 33; 13:3,
7), yet in the time of Joash and Jeroboam II all the
conquered territory had been retaken, so that the
kingdom was not at all restricted in extent. Note
II Kings 13:23-25; 14:26-28. This cannot refer
to the ten tribes, then, in the time of Jeroboam II.
The reference is to the coming judgment in which
Israel will be reduced to a remnant. Isaiah speaks
of the remnant from Judah in 6:13. For thoughts
similar to those in verses 14 and 15 of this chapter
see Isaiah 1:16, 17.

The Blow Has Fallen

The judgment implied in verse 15 is now stated.
In the light of verses 7, 10, 12 and because God
knew that they would not repent, He proclaims the
visitation. The combination of the names of God in
verse 16 is unusual. The mourning will be universal: in the country and field as well as in the city,
death will strike. The city dweller will find the dead
in all the streets, and the farmer will be called from
the field to mourn for someone dead in his home.
The professional mourners, who for hire displayed
excessive grief (Jeremiah 9:17-19), would find
ample employment. The death wail will even pene-
trate the vineyards where ordinarily only the sound
of rejoicing is heard. God would pass through the
land. Compare Exodus 12:12. In Egypt it was a
miraculous infliction of punishment; here in Israel
it will be by the hand of the Assyrian.

The Day of the Lord

Amos now turns to those who desire the day of the Lord and pronounces woe upon them. There are some who see in this group scoffers (Isaiah 5:19; Jeremiah 17:15) who defiantly dare the Lord to do His worst. While this is certainly a possible explanation of the passage, we prefer to see here those who speak piously in the midst of their wicked actions. They are self-deceived hypocrites. In the midst of all their sin they still desired the day of the Lord, because they thought the day would mean glory and victory and deliverance for all Israel regardless of their heart relationship to God. The prophet explains that the day of the Lord is a time of darkness for the wicked (Joel 2:2), and not one of bright hope. They had completely misconceived the nature of the Day of Jehovah. In any event judgment is inescapable. When they seek the day of the Lord as an escape from their present troubles, they are going from one danger to a worse one. Amos in his rustic way pictures one escaping a disaster and then another, only to fall into a third and fatal one. The man who safely escaped the lion does so only to be met by a bear whom he evades only to be mortally bitten by a serpent in the crevice of the wall in his own home when he leans to catch his breath. Inevitable doom, and no bright prospect, will be the portion of the ungodly in that time.

Vain Worship and God's Sentence

If they still expect their worship to stand them in good stead, they are deceived for God hates and despises every detail of it. The divine abhorrence and

disgust are emphatically expressed by the different
terms showing God's vehement displeasure. We are
reminded of a similar indictment of Israel's worship
in Isaiah 1:10 ff. It is not, let it be remembered,
that God had not instituted the sacrificial ritual, but
He could not abide it when the heart was not right.
All the feasts, the solemn assemblies, the burnt offerings, the meal offerings, and the peace offerings
roused the wrath of God. He commands them to
remove the noise of their songs, a contemptuous ap-
praisal of the songs played at the festivals by the
Levites in the temple worship when the sacrifices
were offered. I Chronicles 16:40-42; 23:5. The
worship at Bethel imitated that at Jerusalem in every
important feature. They are advised to incorporate
in their spiritual life those elements so sorely needed
—justice and righteousness. In abundant and perennial measure they are to find their place in the
spiritual life stream of the nation; only then will God
be satisfied. See I Samuel 15:22; Psalm 66:18;
Hosea 6:6; and Micah 6:8 for this vital truth.
Among the most difficult verses in the prophecy of
Amos are verses 25 and 26 of this chapter, and they
have been variously interpreted. Good men are divided as to the answer to the question in verse 25:
some say the answer expected is an affirmative one,
while others claim it is negative. In this controversy
the record in the books of Moses must be decisive.
There we find (Exodus 24:4, 5; Numbers 7:1 ff.;
19:1 ff.) that Israel very definitely and on more
than one occasion offered sacrifices and offerings to
God in the wilderness. It may be true that, once the
generation in the wilderness was sentenced to die,

6

they did so only half-heartedly or even intermit-
tently, yet we cannot give a negative answer to the
· question of Amos. Says the prophet: "Yes, you did
offer to the Lord, and yet you have borne the images
also which you made of your gods." Thus Amos is
charging Israel with observing the ritual of the Mosaic law at the same time that they followed idols,
just as the contemporaries of the prophet in the
northern kingdom were doing. Israel from time
immemorial had given herself to idolatry, and hoped
at the same time that God would be pleased with her
perfunctory round of ritual in the temple. The two
things were incompatible in Moses' time as they were
in Amos' day. Their calf worship at Dan and Bethel
was only the emergence of the idolatry of the calf in
the wilderness. God's judicial sentence on this spiritual monstrosity is exile. The whole kingdom was
to go into captivity beyond Damascus, clearly a reference to Assyria.

Seek God and Live!

Seek God and live! In order to know the will of
God this hour Israel must have the message of the
gospel of her Messiah, the Lord Jesus Christ, pro-
claimed to her in order that by faith she may seek
God and live. They cannot hear without a preacher.

Seek God and live! This is the very message
which all the prophets of the Old Testament sought
to convey to Israel from hearts touched with the love
of God. It is an abiding message and an all-sufficient
one.

Seek God and live! These words are the embodi-
ment of the good news which faithful missionaries

the world over are striving to implant in the hearts
of the lost sheep of the house of Israel while a crazed
and Satan-driven world seeks to drive Israel from
the face of the earth into a Christless eternity. Shall
we not all, everyone of us who names the name of
Christ the Lord, uphold the hands and ministry of
these dear ones as they bear the torch of life to those
who sit in unbelievable darkness and despair? May
God Himself stir us up to do so by word of mouth,
prayer, witness, and sacrifice.

QUESTIONS ON CHAPTER V

1. Are God's dealings with Israel ever so concluded that He no longer concerns Himself about
them?

2. What is the subject of the prophet's lamentation
at the beginning of this chapter?

3. Does Amos prophesy that Israel shall never rise
again? Give proof for your answer.

4. Is hope held out to the ungodly in their wayward condition?

5. Explain the allusions to Bethel, Gilgal, and
Beersheba..

6. What special group is singled out for condemnation and what is their offence?

7. What judgment is foretold for the unjust judges
of Israel?

8. Outline the elements in the entreaty of the
prophet to the people.

9. To whom does the "remnant of Joseph" refer?
Present evidence for your position.

10. Describe the visitation of the Lord spoken of
in verses 16 and 17.

11. Will the Day of the Lord be a boon and blessing to all Israel?

12. How does Amos picture the inescapable doom?

13. Did God disapprove of the whole Levitical system with its offerings and holy days? Explain.

14. What elements are dearer to God than mere ritual and form?

15. Discuss fully verses 25 and 26, giving reasons for your position.

16. What is God's insistent entreaty to Israel today?

17. Where does the child of God fit into this program for Israel?

Chapter VI

"AT EASE IN ZION"

Woe to the Godless Leaders

THE chapter begins with a "woe" which relates this portion to the woe pronounced in 5:18. It is pronounced upon those who are at ease in Zion. They are resting in a false security engendered by a heartless ritual and worship which they blindly believe will satisfy God. Thus they live in a reckless and careless manner. What was true of those living in Zion was equally applicable to those who considered themselves secure in the mountain of Samaria. Nature had wonderfully endowed the city of Samaria with fortifications, indeed, of such a character that the Assyrian king could not take it before three years of siege. II Kings 17:5, 6. Both parts of the nation, Judah and Israel, are here in view, although the latter is emphasized in what follows. "At ease in Zion"—what a vivid designation for those who are indifferent while in a place of privilege and rich blessing! It is the condition of too many in the Church today with no care for the lost sheep outside the flock of Christ, least of all for the lost sheep of the house of Israel. God never intended us to be heedlessly and indulgently at ease in our favored position of truth and light in Christ the Lord. The indictment of Amos is laid at the door of the notable leaders of the nation which is here designated as the chief of the nations. Their nation held a privileged and exalted position as the peculiar and chosen people of the Lord. To the godless and careless heads of this chosen nation the people of Israel came for justice, help, and for the settlement of their controversies. The people come to their leaders, but they have a care only for self-indulgence, ease, and revelry. The prophet now tells them to consider carefully Calneh, which was built by Nimrod in the land of Shinar (Genesis 10: 10; Isaiah 10: 9; and probably Ezekiel 27: 23) on the east bank of the Tigris River, although some identify it with Kullani, a few miles from Arpad; Hamath, the chief city of Syria which was situated on the Orontes River, later called Epiphania; and Gath, the principal city of Philistia. Why are these cities pointed out by the prophet? We know that they were cities of spiritual corruption, but the prophet does not emphasize this fact. Some think the verse is understandable only if these kingdoms were on the decline. For Gath we are directed to 1: 8 where it is not even mentioned among the cities that comprise Philistia. Calneh, too, is said to have lost its independence early and have been annexed to the Assyrian Empire. Hamath was subdued by Jeroboam II (II Kings 14: 25) and then by Assyria (II Kings 18: 34). These could not ward off the enemy, then how do you expect to? If they experienced the judgment of God for their heathen ways, how can guilty Judah and Israel escape similar chastisement from the Lord? All about her God's people could see warning signs in the fate of other godless nations. See Nahum 3: 8. While such a view is entirely possible, we believe the prophet is probably pointing to the aforementioned nations and asking whether they (the nations) were better than these kingdoms (Judah and Israel)? The answer is negative, for none of the surrounding nations was comparable to Israel. Amos shows that they are rightly called the chief of the nations, because they are not lacking in greatness to any of the prosperous nations about her, in fact, excels them. Their border was not greater than that of the people of God. The prophet says, Look at these others and see just how favored (chief) you are.

Luxury and Sin

Being chief of the nations how did Israel respond to the favor and blessing of God? With aversion and with desire to avoid the wrath of God they put far away the evil day, the day of God's punishment for their evil deeds. Compare Ezekiel 12: 22, 27. When men put off the day of God's reckoning, they always feel free to indulge themselves in all manner of violence. So it was in Israel. Note Ecclesiastes 8: 11 for this important truth. The violence was manifested most clearly by the sitting of the unjust judges in judgment. While these judges were harsh in judging others, they were soft, indulgent, and licentious. Stretching themselves full length (so the original) on beds inlaid with ivory, they feasted to their hearts' content on the choicest and fattest of meats. Self-indulgence was given free rein. Here was extravagant and careless living in the midst of oppression and poverty. Indulgence of every appetite was the order of the day. And what would revelling be without song and wine? In Samaria they were not lacking either. Their songs were idle songs;

they were mere nonsense. The drunkard is known by his song. The ungodly leaders in Israel devised instruments of music for their special occasions and feastings. In this they were paralleling the genius of David, the great master musician of Israel. His ability was directed toward the praise of God; theirs was employed to celebrate the impious revelries in which they were engaged. David honored God with his music; they dishonored both God and man. Music which is degrading is a sure sign of an incipient national decline. How we need to heed this word in our own land! See Nehemiah 12:36 for the prowess of David in music. The hours of debauchery would not be complete if wine did not find its place among the celebrants. The regular cups were insufficient for their insatiable appetites, so they drank wine from bowls. It is the same word as for the bowls used for sacrificial purposes to catch the blood and then sprinkle it. Numbers 7:13. When they should have been sitting in sackcloth and ashes over the affliction of their people, that is, the low spiritual condition of the kingdom, they were anointing themselves with the most costly oils instead. In time of mourning (see II Samuel 14:2) anointing was suspended.

Captivity Foretold

Those who were first in prominence and sin will be the first in punishment and captivity. Going with the first captives will make their shame all the more conspicuous. The revelry, the discordant noises and screeching, of the carousers will pass away. The Lord swears by Himself (compare 4:2) that. since

He abhors and hates the excellency of Jacob and his palaces, He will deliver over the entire city with all it possesses to the hand of the enemy. In Hosea 5:5 the word translated here "excellency" means pride or arrogance; in Amos 8:7 it clearly refers to God Himself as the object of Israel's glorying. In our text here it must refer, as being parallel to palaces, to the sanctuary and all that constituted the glory of the nation Israel. See Psalm 47:4 and Ezekiel 24: 21. The palaces, which were places of corruption and storehouses of plunder from the poor (3:10, 15), would suffer the stroke of God also. In the next two verses we are given a vivid picture of the plague such as usually followed war in the East, as elsewhere even to modern times. The prophet desires to show the comprehensive sweep of the judgment, so he assumes a house in which ten men live, and states that they shall all die. The number is a round number (Leviticus 26:26; Zechariah 8:23) but indicates a large house. What a fearful contrast, then, do we have here to the conditions portrayed in verses 4 to 6 of this chapter. There we have pictured for us luxury, licentiousness, and indifference, while here we have fear, stark tragedy, and universal death. How widespread the plague will be is noted for us in verse 10. When one's next of kin, to whom the duty of burial belonged, would come to carry the corpse out of the house to burn it, he would find but one remaining out of the ten who lived there formerly. And that last surviving one hidden away in the innermost recesses of the houses fearfully awaiting the hour when the plague would carry him away also. In ancient Israel in accordance with the

words of Genesis 3:19 burial was the accepted
method of disposal of the dead. In this the New
Testament doctrine of the body concurs. Hence cremation was considered wrong and not countenanced
(see Amos 2:1). But when God's judgment falls
upon His people, there will be so many dead that
they will not bury but burn them. The cases here
and I Samuel 31:12 are exceptional cases. Here
cremation is resorted to in order to prevent contagion;
in I Samuel it was done to obviate further dishonor
of the bodies of Saul and his sons by the Philistines.
When asked if there are others alive, the remaining
occupant of the house will say there is none. Immediately he will be told to hold his peace for fear he
would mention the name of the Lord in announcing
the death of the others in the household, or in prais-
ing God for his own deliverance. Punishment will
so work fear and despair in them all that they will
refrain from even the mention of the name of the
Lord (which should be their sole refuge in such an
hour) lest further wrath come upon them. By the
command of the Lord both the great house and the
small house will be smitten. From early times it has
been suggested that the great house refers to the
kingdom of the ten tribes and the small house to the
kingdom of the two tribes. Although it is true that
the Assyrians did break up the first and begin the
work of destruction in 'the second, it is better to see
here a reference to the judgment of God which will
touch the homes of the rich and poor alike. See
3:15.

False Confidence

Amos would now show how impossible it is for

them in their sinful state to expect the protection, prospering, or blessing of God. Taking a figure from the realm of the rustic, he asks whether it is customary for horses to run upon a rock, or whether oxen are used there to plow. This is no more possible than that their evil deeds should issue in their blessing. How can they expect the favor of the Lord at the very time they are committing deeds displeasing to God? It is as absurd as trying to run horses on rocks. Those who have delighted in unjust judgment, turning justice and righteousness into gall and wormwood, have prided themselves in and boasted themselves of that which is truly nothing, namely, their boasted strength. They have vaunted themselves that they have gotten them horns (a figure in Scripture for power which it is to a number of animals) by their own strength. To what is the reference made? We have doubtless a reference to the military resources of Jeroboam II in which the kingdom of Israel was vainly trusting. Theirs was a false security doomed to catastrophe. Again Amos foretells the coming of the nation which is the rod of God's chastisement for Israel, namely, Assyria, but the name is not given. The Assyrian army will do an effective work on Israel for they will smite the kingdom in its entire extent, from the entrance of Hamath, the pass between the Lebanons, to the brook of the Arabah, the Kidron. The latter was the southern boundary of the ten tribes, and falls into the Dead Sea south of Jericho. The prophet began the chapter with the pronouncement of woe, and concludes it with the execution of that woe.

"At Ease in Zion"

Dear reader, do you think that the heart of the blessed Saviour was at rest in Zion when He looked on that city and wept? Do you consider that His heart is satisfied now with the desperate spiritual condition of Zion? How can we be so at ease in Zion, in the place of privilege and blessing, when Israel is dying without the knowledge of Him who is their life and light and eternal glory? The Lord continues throughout the days, months, and years so rapidly passing to woo us to carry forward this service so near and dear to His heart. Writ large on the heart of the Saviour is the word "Zion." Is it on yours?

QUESTIONS ON CHAPTER VI

1. How does Amos describe the reckless ease of his contemporaries?

2. What contributed to this feeling of carnal security?

3. How does "at ease in Zion" fit conditions in the Church today?

4. Why does Amos point out Calneh, Hamath, and Gath? Explain.

5. How did Israel respond to the blessing of God?

6. Why did the ungodly seek to put off the evil day of judgment?

7. Portray the wicked life of the ungodly judges in Israel.

8. How are the ungodly leaders contrasted with godly David?

9. Did the lamentable condition of the people concern the wicked judges? Explain.

10. How does Amos foretell the captivity?

11. Describe the ravages of the plague.

12. How do you interpret verse 10?

13. Discuss the Biblical viewpoint on burial of the dead.

14. What are the interpretations of verse 11? What is your explanation?

15. Explain the figure from nature in verse 12.

16. To what is reference made in the horns of verse 13?

17. Was our Lord Jesus Christ ever "at ease in Zion"?

18. Dare we be at ease over the condition of Zion now?

Chapter VII

GOD'S WORD AND MAN'S OPPOSITION

The Vision of the Locusts

THIS chapter begins the third division of the book: (1) oracles of judgment on the nations, chapters 1 and 2; (2) threatening prophecies on Israel, chapters 3 to 6; and (3) a series of five visions of judgment, concluding with ultimate blessing. The first four visions have practically the same introductory formula. See 7:1, 4, 7, and 8:1. There are some students of this prophecy who understand these visions to speak figuratively of the three invasions of the Assyrians under Pul, Tiglath-pileser, and finally Shalmaneser. But the form of the visions and the context would lead us to take the visions as representing actual occurrences in the corporate life of Israel. Nor are the judgments portrayed in the first two visions prospective; they are better considered as actual and taking place in the time and hour in which Amos was prophesying and ministering. Amos was shown the Lord as He was forming locusts to plague the land after the king's mowings at the beginning of the shooting up of the latter growth. This is not necessarily the same plague mentioned in chapter 4, for locust plagues are frequent in Palestine, occurring about every seven years. The king's mowings evidently refer to the tribute which the people paid to the king from the first harvest. Compare I Kings 4:7 ff. and 18:5.

In Palestine two crops a year were usual. Since the
first mowings were the king's, the people depended
of necessity upon the second crop for their own sus-
tenance, and it was this harvest which was threatened
by the locust plague sent by God. God uses nature
in His moral government of His people for their
correction. The language of verse 2 would appear
to preclude the conclusion that the locusts here speak
of an invading army as they do in the prophecy of
Joel; however, some do so interpret it. When the
locusts had consumed all the grass of the land, the
prophet betook himself to intercessory prayer. Prayer
alone could divert the disaster, and the man of God
prays that the people may be forgiven. Else how
could the nation, helpless and enfeebled, hope to en-
dure in its insignificant condition? We need not wonder at the extreme condition in which Israel is portrayed in this verse for a locust plague is a calamity
of great proportions. Amos pleads in such a way
as to touch the heart of God with the plight of His
people, and He is entreated for them. How we do
well to learn this lesson! God wants us to pray for
His lost ones in Israel and He promises to hear and
answer abundantly with life and salvation. Paul
knew the wisdom of it (Romans 10:1). The
prophets were ever touched with the need of God's
people. Note Isaiah 51:19; also Psalm 106:44, 45.
At the intercession of Amos the Lord repented Himself and stayed the plague. Prayer had made it possible for God justly to spare Israel in answer to it.
Many have wondered how it could ever be said that
God repents (Numbers 23:19; James 1:17), but it
is more in the way of the language of appearance.

We must remember that God ever works in accordance with His infinite holiness and righteousness. When sin is present God must condemn and punish it; when prayer and the grace of God operate to provide a way of escape then God spares. In each case He is working in the strictest conformity with His known holiness. Thus it was that in answer to trusting prayer God said He would not allow the plague to ravage any longer. Only eternity will reveal fully how much in the plan of God has been wrought through consistent and persistent prayer for the salvation of souls in Israel and throughout the world.

The Vision of the Fire

When Israel continued in their sinful ways though they had been spared in the grace of God, He determined to send upon them another visitation. In the second vision Amos sees the Lord calling fire into His service in order to punish His people. The fire referred to is doubtless drought. See 4:6-11. In the early part of the prophecy it had reference to war as in 1:4 and succeeding passages. In a coming day the Lord will punish again by fire (Isaiah 66: 16). The drought was so severe that it is represented as devouring the great deep, a designation for the ocean which feeds the earth with springs of water. Compare Genesis 7:11; 49:25; Isaiah 51:10. The land also, that is, the portion of Israel, was threatened. Micah 2:4. This grievous stroke calls forth the prayer of Amos once more, and he beseeches the Lord to cease because of the miserable condition of Israel. Again the Lord, who loves to be entreated of His own and for His own, heard and removed the distress. Thus Amos would show that the Lord was not bent on destroying Israel, but on turning her from her evil ways by disciplinary judgments. How well these threatenings achieved their objective we shall see in the next vision.

The Vision of the Plumb-line

In the last vision of this chapter Amos is shown the Lord as He stands beside (or over) a wall made by a plumb-line, that is, a perpendicular wall. In His hand He has a plumb-line which is clearly to be put to use to test how true and straight the wall is. Just as the builder uses the plumb-line for testing, God will exercise His unerring standard to test the spiritual integrity of His people. The Scriptures reveal that the plumb-line was employed not only in building houses, but in destroying as well. In this passage the Lord has destruction in mind as is clear from verses 8 and 9. Note carefully II Kings 21: 13; Isaiah 28: 17; 34: 11; Lamentations 2: 8. The plumb-line is set in the midst of Israel, not merely on the circumference of the nation. This will be a thoroughgoing judgment, and the Lord warns that He will not again pass by, forgive, them. There is no intercession from the prophet here, for the patience of God is at an end. Now nothing can stay the oncoming catastrophe. More than once the intercession of the prophet had averted the blow from the Lord's hand, but that hour was passed. We next learn of what the judgment will consist: the high places will be made desolate, the sanctuaries will be destroyed, and the house of Jeroboam will be cut off by the sword. The high places were the groves

7

where idols were worshipped, and the sanctuaries
are those set up originally by Jeroboam the son of
Nebat at Dan and Bethel. The name Isaac is used
here instead of Israel as a name for the ten tribes.
Both the false worship and the ungodly monarchy in
Israel will be swept away. Amos does not declare
that Jeroboam will perish by the sword (which was
not true, see II Kings 14:23-29), but that God
would rise against the house of Jeroboam with the
sword which was fulfilled in the assassination of his
son Zechariah by Shallum. II Kings 15:8-10. In
the next generation the name of Jeroboam was cut
off. How sure are the mercies of God and how certain are His judgments!

False Priest Versus God's Prophet

Such straightforward proclamation of the will and
purpose of God is ever displeasing to the unregen-
erate and ungodly man. And so it was in the day of
Amos. The Word of God did not go unchallenged.
Amaziah, who was the high priest at the sanctuary
of the golden calf in Bethel, accused the prophet before Jeroboam. Note the particulars of his indictment: first, he claims that Amos has conspired
against the king himself, implying others were with
the prophet in a plot; second, that the conspiracy
was being perpetrated in the very midst of the house
of Israel, at the religious center of the kingdom at
Bethel; lastly, that the land could not suffer the
prophesying of Amos. Ungodly Amaziah begins
with the baseless charge of treason and concludes
with the alarming word that revolution or sedition
may result from the prophet's words. It was an un-

intentional testimony to the power of God's Word
when it comes to convict or correct, or indeed at any
time.   Political expediency in every age dishonors
and opposes the testimony of the truth.   Note Elijah
(I Kings 18: 17) ; Jeremiah (Jeremiah 37: 13-15) ;
our Lord Jesus (John 19: 12) ; the disciples (John
11: 48-50) ; and Paul (Acts 17: 6, 7).   In verse 11
we have the manner in which a hireling and time-
server can twist the simple words of a servant of
God.   Amaziah distorts the words of Amos so that
they appear to be a personal charge against the king.
There is no mention of any action of the king against
the prophet.   The false priest omits the basis of the
threat, the hope held out by the prophet for the people in the event of repentance (5: 4, 6), and the
prophet's own intercession for the kingdom.   Now
Amaziah addresses himself to Amos and calling him
seer with contemptuous reference to his visions, ad-
vises the prophet to flee to his own country in Judah
and there prophesy for his living, his bread.   He in-
sinuated that Amos ministered for the sake of his
livelihood.   The king's priest was himself a hireling
and intimates that God's prophet is also.   He further
enjoins upon Amos that he prophesy no more at
Bethel, because it was a royal sanctuary and royal
residence.   I Kings 12: 28.   Man-made religion cannot abide the truth of God.   Mark that Amaziah does
not call Bethel and its sanctuary the house or sanctuary of God.   It is the king's.   Unwittingly he truth-
fully lays bare the human origin of the entire worship
of the Israelitish kingdom begun by Jeroboam I and
carried on by his godless successors.   Amos is told
(2: 12) that his ministry at Bethel must be discon-

tinued, because the city was the seat of the religion
of the kingdom as well as one of the king's residences.

Amos' Defence and Israel's Doom

Amos' only defence, and altogether adequate it is
too, is a simple statement of how God called His
servant to the work of the prophet. Amos denies
that he is a professional prophet or that he was
taught in the schools of the prophets where young
men were trained for instructing the nation. I Samuel
19:24. He was pursuing his humble occupation as
a herdsman and dresser of sycamore trees when God's
unmistakable call came to him to prophesy to Israel.
His word and his authority were not his own, but
derived directly from God. See Galatians 1:1; also
II Samuel 7:8 where we have similar words in the
case of David's call to the royal office. In short,
Amos is saying he must obey God rather than man.
Acts 5:29. Note the contrasts in verse 11: "thus
Amos saith" and in verse 16: "Thou sayest" and in
verse 17: "thus saith Jehovah." Amos is pointing
out as a true prophet that it matters not what Amaziah says nor what he, Amos, says, but it is all important to hear what God the Lord says. No man's
opposition can stay the mighty onsweep of the majestic Word of God. One of the early Christian
writers said: "Heaven thundered and commanded
him to prophesy; the frog croaked in answer out of
his marsh, *prophesy no more.*" Instead of Amaziah's harangue against Amos stopping the mouth
of the prophet, it brought the judgment nearer home.
The prophecy now names him individually. In the
invasion of the land by the enemy the wife of the

false priest would be publicly ravished; his sons and daughters would be slain; his land would be portioned out; and he himself would die in an unclean land (Assyria) whither Israel would be carried captive. With this final prophecy Amos shows the dire consequences of opposition to the truth on individual and nation alike. It is a fearful thing to set one's self against the truth of God. If man tries to silence it, it cries out the louder.

"How Shall Jacob Stand?"

These words were the burden of the prayer of Amos when Israel was facing only physical and political disaster. But I am deeply stirred as I think of the lost condition of Israel without the knowledge of the Lord Jesus Christ, their Messiah and Saviour, attempting to abide the soul-searching scrutiny of the Lord in the day of judgment for the lost. Without the Saviour, I beg you, how, how shall Jacob stand? He cannot. Let us hasten by the grace of God to give them the gospel so they can stand on the Rock of Ages!

QUESTIONS ON CHAPTER VII

1. Give the threefold division of Amos' prophecy.

2. Of what do the visions speak in general?

3. Describe the first vision and give its intended meaning.

4. By what means was the calamity averted?

5. What does the Bible mean when it speaks of God as repenting?

6. What was the second vision? What did it import?

7. Explain the third vision. What did it mean?

8. What punishment is indicated for the house of Jeroboam? Who are involved in this visitation?

9. Describe fully the conflict between Amaziah and Amos. What was the issue at stake?

10. Illustrate how political expediency has opposed the truth of God in several instances.

11. Indicate the number of telling admissions in the accusation of Amaziah.

12. What was Amos' defence of his ministry? Upon what basic fact was the prophet ultimately depending?.

13. What was the effect of Amaziah's opposition in the end?

14. Can Israel stand in the hour and day of judgment without salvation in the Saviour?

15. How can we provide by grace a standing place for them?

Chapter VIII
FAMINE OF GOD'S WORD

The Vision of the Basket of Fruit

AT THE beginning of the eighth chapter of Amos we have the fourth vision in the series shown the prophet by the Lord. The vision of the plumbline showed the certainty of the coming judgment; this vision reveals the nearness of that visitation. The prophet sees a basket of ripe fruit and the Lord explains that this indicates Israel is ripe for judgment. Just as the gathering of fruit marked the end of the harvest, so Israel had come to the end of their national existence. Since the providential dealings of the Lord, His threatenings, His promises, and His early chastenings had not issued in true penitence, the hour for judgment had arrived for the northern kingdom. There is a forceful play on words in this vision: "summer fruit" (*qayits*) and "end" (*qets*). See Joel 3:13 and Ezekiel 7:2, 3, 6. The words "I will not again pass by them," meaning that the Lord will not again forgive them, resume the thought of judgment in Amos' prophecies, interrupted by the accusation and opposition of Amaziah. Compare 7:8. Because the same Hebrew word is sometimes translated "temple" and at other times "palace," students of verse 3 have differed as to which songs are referred to, whether those of the temple or those of the palace. Both are referred to in this book—temple songs in 5:23 and songs in the palace in 6:5

and probably 8:10. The important feature is that
they will not be silenced merely, but will be changed
into howlings and wailings because of the ravages of
death on every hand. The dead bodies will be so
numerous that they will be cast forth in every place
in an indiscriminate manner. While occupied thus
they are commanded to silence: "Hush!" It is the
same charge to silence as in 6:10; it is an exhortation to submit beneath the severity of the judgment
of God. The grief is so great that words are utterly
useless. Why resort to words when the slaughter is
so vast that the customary rites of burial cannot be
performed? Truly, Israel was ripe for judgment and
that stroke was not far off.

Warnings to the Oppressors of the Poor

Amos now directs a scathing rebuke against those
who enrich themselves at the expense of the poor.
If they could, they would swallow up the needy (2:
6, 7) and cause them to cease from the land altogether. See Isaiah 5:8. Their covetous spirits took
the joy out of the feasts and sabbaths because, although they observed them in a perfunctory way,
they were continually thinking only of the end of
these sacred days when they could give themselves
again to their relentless pursuit of material gain. The
new moon was a holy day on which business and
trade were not transacted. The sabbath, of course,
was a day on which such pursuits could not be carried on. Compare Numbers 10:10; 28:11; II Kings
4:23; and Nehemiah 10:31; 13:15-18. The mention of new moon and sabbath is another indication
in this book that, while the people were keeping the

rounds of idol worship, they were practising the appointments of the Mosaic law as well. Those who have no real piety have no honesty either. Thus we find these oppressors not giving the proper weight in food, while they increase the price. (In those days money was weighed out, Jeremiah 32:9). The law had forbidden both these dishonest practices. See Deuteronomy 25:13-16. Every transaction was marked by fraud and dishonesty. The poor were ultimately reduced to slavery. For the least amount the needy had to sell themselves into slavery. Leviticus 25:39 prohibited such dealings. And that which an honest dealer throws away, the refuse of the wheat, they sold. Grievous as these conditions are, they are not without parallel many times over in our own day. The Scriptures indicate that similar conditions will prevail in Christendom before the return of the Lord. Note James 5:1-6.

The Comprehensive Judgment

As the prophet begins to describe the many-sided judgment on the people of God, he states the fearful truth that the Lord has sworn by the excellency of Jacob, that is, by Himself (as in 4:2 and 6:8), that He will never forget any of their works. They had heaped up sins unto the day of wrath and God was mindful of every one of them committed. Only God's glorious provision in grace can blot out the memory of any sin before the Lord. So great will be the impact of the judgment from the Lord that the land will tremble, all the inhabitants of the land will mourn, and the land itself will rise and sink like the Nile, the river of Egypt. Some understand the verse to be speaking of an earthquake, but the thought is rather that the land will shake from the weight of the judgment it is called upon to bear. The same concept recurs in 9:5, but there it is introduced to show the omnipotence of God. In that same day of chastisement the sun will go down at noon and the earth will be darkened in a clear day. It has been suggested that the reference is to an eclipse of the sun. This could hardly be a description of an eclipse even from the viewpoint of the language of appearance. Could this be an allusion to the terrible day of the Lord? A comparison of this passage with Joel 2:2; 3:15; and Matthew 24:29-30 will readily show that such phenomena will take place in the day of tribulation and judgment. But many epoch-making events in the Bible have their foreshadowings in previous historical events, and this may be just such an instance. For example, this expression is employed when one is destroyed in the midst of prosperity. It is a metaphorical setting forth of the change from prosperity to extreme adversity. Not only will earth and heavens be affected by the comprehensive judgment, but all the inhabitants of the land. The feasts in Israel were always occasions for great joy and rejoicing, but now they shall be turned into mourning and their songs into weeping. See Hosea 2:11. Sackcloth on all loins (Ezekiel 7:18) and baldness on every head (Isaiah 3:24 and Jeremiah 16:6) are alike marks of deepest mourning. Theirs will be as the mourning for an only son, the one in whom the family name was to be perpetuated. Joel 1:8 gives us a related figure, while Jeremiah 6:26 and Zechariah 12:10 have the identical picture.

Just as in Egypt of old there was mourning in every house for the dead (Exodus 12:30), so similar conditions would now obtain in Israel under the heavy judgment of the Lord. Nor will the trouble be a transitory or a temporary one, but a sorrow that would continue on in its bitterness.

Famine of the Word of God

Another phase of the judgment of the Lord must be set forth before Amos presents the last vision in the concluding chapter of the prophecy. The distress of the people will be outward and inward, temporal and spiritual. Their spiritual plight is depicted in terms of a famine, but not a famine for bread nor thirst for water; rather it will be a famine of hearing the words of the Lord. What can this mean? The Old Testament Scriptures reveal clearly enough how God in His boundless love for Israel sent them messages through His servants to draw them back into the path of His choosing and into conformity with His will for them. But these prophets and servants were opposed; their messages were scorned; and they were told to cease their ministrations. Now the Lord tells them that, since they despised His Word through the prophets when it was brought to them, they were to know the cessation of all prophetic communication. Note Ezekiel 7:26 and Micah 3:7. The Word of the Lord will be withdrawn from them. Like disobedient Saul in the hour of his extremity (I Samuel 28:6), they will seek after the Lord in order to obtain relief from physical distress and consolation for their troubled hearts. This is divine retribution for such opposition to the truth as seen

in 7:12, 13. Compare also for the same principle
of divine dealing Luke 17:22 and John 7:34; 8:21.
How perverse is the nature of man: when he has the
Word of God he despises it; when it is withheld he
seeks it because of the severity of the chastisement.
The widespread restlessness and dissatisfaction incident upon the Lord's act of judgment are portrayed
vividly in verse 12. The distraught people will
wander from sea to sea in every direction seeking
the Word of God and will not find it. They will reel
like a drunkard or the swaying of trees in the wind.
The position has been taken that the directions given
in this verse refer to the extent of the land of Palestine, that is, from the Mediterranean to the Dead Sea.
In view of the indefinite language of the verse and its
affinity to such passages as Psalm 72:8 and Zechariah 9:10, probably every quarter of the globe is intended by the prophet. It has been well said: "He
that will not when he may, when he will shall have
nay." So with Israel in the hour of judgment; they
will seek the Word of Jehovah but will not find it.
Of the entire population those are now singled out
who are the strongest and the most buoyant with
hope—the fair virgins and the young men. But
these too will lack all consolation; they shall faint
for thirsting after the Word. If this be true of the
young and vigorous (Isaiah 40:30, 31), what of the
aged and feeble? What is true of them is all the
more so for the rest whom they represent. Finally,
Amos assigns once more the reason for the conditions
envisioned in verses 11 to 13. In short, they were
so taken up with the false gods that they could no
longer hear the Word of the true and living God.

They had forsaken the Lord and He now forsakes
them. It was their practice to swear in the name of
their gods. God had charged them to swear in the
name of the Lord (Deuteronomy 6: 13; 10: 20), not
in that of other gods (Joshua 23: 7). By the sin of
Samaria the golden calf at Bethel is meant. See 4: 4
and Hosea 8: 5. The god of Dan was evidently the
bull image set up by Jeroboam the son of Nebat.
I. Kings 12: 29 ff. The way of Beersheba (5: 5) was
the last of the three oaths made in the names of the
three idol sanctuaries. Swearing in the name of in-
animate objects may be strange to us, but not so in
the Orient. Mohammedans are accustomed to swearing "by the pilgrimage" to Mecca, as well as in the
name of countless other objects that may come to
mind at the time of the oath. All these oaths were
after the form which the Lord Himself had instituted: "As the Lord liveth!" It is appropriate for
the Lord because in Him is life and He exists. It is
senseless when employed of idols which represent
no living entity. Paul's estimate (through the Spirit
of God) of idols is the only true one: "we know that
no idol is anything in the world" or as the newest
translation of the New Testament puts it: "we know
that an idol has no real existence." I Corinthians
8: 4. The doom upon them for such idolatry is
tersely stated; they shall fall and never rise again
(see 5: 2). The fulfillment of this word began with
the dissolution of the kingdom of Israel and continues until their national restoration which is promised in such passages as Ezekiel 36: 22-31 and 37:
15-23. The partial fulfillment in the time of the
Assyrian captivity points on to the ultimate fulfill-

ment in the period before the visible return of the
Lord in glory. Apostate Christendom, as well as
guilty Israel, will share this famine in the time of
Great Tribulation. Both have turned now from the
light of the truth to the darkness of fables.

"Shall Seek . . . Shall Not Find"

These are indeed sad words and speak of a woeful
condition. But thank God it is not true for any lost
soul in Israel now. It cannot be said they shall seek
now and shall not find the Lord. The gospel of
God's grace in their Messiah is meant for them now
and whosoever among them shall call upon the name
of the Lord shall be saved. Romans 10:13. God
asks us to make this blessed message available to
them. It is our rich and joyous privilege to see that
this word of truth and invitation unto salvation
reaches them through called and devoted servants of
the Lord. We dare not pass by the opportunity. Let
us buy it up.

QUESTIONS ON CHAPTER VIII

1. Relate the fourth vision of this book to that of
the previous three.

2. What does the prophet see? What does it
mean?

3. What judgment is foretold?

4. What picture does Amos give of the oppressors
of the needy?

5. Were the appointments of the Mosaic law done
away with while the ungodly pursued their selfish
devices? Explain.

6. Show from Scripture the parallel to these conditions in the latter days of the Church age.

7. Describe the several features of the judgment foretold here.

8. Indicate how the distress of the people will be both outward and inward.

9. What is meant by a famine of hearing the words of the Lord? Illustrate.

10. Explain "the sin of Samaria."

11. What was the god of Dan? Why does Amos speak of the "way of Beersheba"?

12. Set forth the time referred to in the judgment just presented by the prophet.

13. Is it true now that any lost soul can seek the Lord and not find Him? Is it applicable to Israel?

14. Prove that God is available for any seeking Israelite in the world today. Give Scripture reference.

Chapter IX

THE RESTORATION OF ISRAEL

The Vision of the Temple Destruction

THE last chapter of the prophecy of Amos concerns itself with the final and consummating vision, that of the destruction of the temple. The scene is in the main sanctuary of the northern kingdom at Bethel, not at Jerusalem. The Lord Himself directs the judgment and commands that the capitals, the tops of the pillars, be smitten, so that the very thresholds may shake. The blow from the top shatters the sanctuary to its foundations. Both top and bottom are mentioned to show the complete destruction. When the pillars come crashing they will fall on the heads of the crowds of people who are evidently gathered in the temple on a festival occasion. They would all be buried in the ruins. In case any should escape the crash of the building they will be slain by the sword. In this vivid manner does the prophet depict the wrath of God upon all the idolatrous worship of Israel and His summary judgment upon it, a judgment without remedy. Twice the word is given that no one will flee the catastrophe. Verses 2 to 4 expand the last thought in verse 1 that there is no possibility of escape. We are given hypothetical cases of attempts at escape from the judgment and the utter inevitability of their doom. In words that strongly remind us of Psalm 139:7-10 Amos sets forth the omnipresence of God. Though the doomed ones dig into the bowels of the earth, into Sheol, there will the mighty hand of God overtake them; should they attempt to ascend the greatest heights, thence will God bring them low. The same is said of Babylon in Jeremiah 51:53 and of Edom in Obadiah 4. It has been well said that "The grave is not so awful as God." The omnipresence of God is a comforting and sustaining truth to the good, but a terror to the wicked when judgment is in view. Even if the fugitives sought to hide themselves in the top of Carmel, it would not avail them against the searching eye of the Lord. Mount Carmel rises quite suddenly out of the sea to a height of about 1,800 feet. It is claimed that there are some 1,000 caves in Carmel, especially on the west side toward the sea. The mountain is known for its dense forests and large caverns, the latter often serving hermits for shelter. Not only will these caverns not suffice for concealment from the wrath of the Lord, but the very bottom of the sea will not afford refuge to those who would escape. At the bottom of the sea the Lord will command the sea-serpent to bite the culprits. Compare Isaiah 27:1. Just as the great fish obeyed the Lord when He commanded it to swallow a Jonah, so the serpent of the sea will do the Lord's bidding with regard to the sinners in Israel. Should the ungodly go into captivity before their enemies, that is, voluntarily in order in this way to spare their lives, even there the sword will destroy them. Assyria is again in view, although not named anywhere in the prophecy. Futile and worse will be all attempts to escape the scourge of God's hand in the day of His fearful visitation. The reason is

8

found in the fact that God has set His eyes with fixed purpose upon them, not as formerly for good and blessing, but for evil only. He has purposed and it will stand; He will watch over it to bring it to pass.

The Omnipotent God

Lest any of his hearers falsely comfort himself that the Lord will not or cannot do what He has threatened, Amos majestically sets forth the omnipotence of our God, the Lord Jehovah of hosts. He is the God of all power (see 4:13; 5:8, 9; and 8:8). Assuredly, power belongs, not to the atom bomb, but to the Lord. The Lord needs only touch the earth in judgment and it is dissolved. Compare Psalm 46:6. God can cause the earth to rise and sink like the Nile of Egypt, and, since He has framed the heavens and the earth, He is able to bring floods upon the earth. All nature is subservient to Him; only man defies His will. Therefore, as in the past so in the future, God will employ the very forces of nature to judge His ungodly creatures. This is clearly pictured for us throughout the Book of Revelation. The prophet Amos is thus asking Israel: "Can you escape such a God?"

Sinners and the Remnant

Carnal reliance upon their election as the people of God will not avert the wrath of God against Israel. In idolatry they had become like the pagan peoples about them. They had lowered themselves to the plane of the heathen, hence they are like the Ethiopians in the sight of the Lord. This is the strongest denunciation of Israel by the prophet, because he likens them to the heathen. Amos shows that since

God in His providential dealings has shifted and
transferred different peoples from their original
homes, Israel need not be illusioned by the notion
that, since He had brought them out of Egypt into
Canaan, they were in such a favored position that
they could never be judged severely for their sins.
Privileges cannot be pleaded in the interests of salvation and deliverance so long as they are scorned
or abused. The Ethiopians had been taken from
their original abode in Arabia and transplanted
among the nations in Africa. The Israelites, after
four centuries of bondage, were delivered out of
Egypt and returned to Canaan. God had brought
the Philistines from Caphtor, probably Crete, although the Greek translators of the Old Testament
thought it was Cappadocia. See Genesis 10:14;
Deuteronomy 2:23; Jeremiah 47:4; and Ezekiel
25:16. According to the Deuteronomy passage it
would appear that this transfer must have taken place
even before the exodus of the people of Israel from
Egypt. Finally, the prophet notes that God had
transplanted the Syrians from Kir to the regions
about Damascus. Compare 1:5. Where, then, was
the occasion for Israel to boast or to rely carnally
upon her privileged position? Again God is seen as
Lord of all the nations as in chapters 1 and 2. And
in all of them alike He must punish sins and de-
partures from Himself. So He declares that His
eyes are upon the sinful kingdom of Ephraim to destroy it from the face of the earth. The words "sinful kingdom" are an unusual designation for the
northern kingdom and how contrary is this condition
to God's ideal for them as stated in Exodus 19:6.

Up to this point in the Book of Amos there has been
no word to mitigate the sentence of judgment. The
prophecy has been singularly free of predictions of
future blessing and prosperity. Now the prophet
states that, although in all justice and holiness God
must destroy forever the northern kingdom, He will
not utterly destroy the house of Jacob, the name for
the whole nation. The reason is given in Jeremiah
31:36. God will not default in His promises to
Abraham and his seed. How the last words of verse
8 are to be understood and carried out is set forth in
verse 9. God will sift (a vivid word which means
"to cause to move to and fro") the house of Israel
among all the nations, as grain in a sieve, yet He will
not allow the smallest kernel to fall to the ground.
Here we have several noteworthy features. First,
it is the Lord who is the moving Agent in all the
sifting. The sifting, in the second place, depicts the
highly unsettled condition of Israel. Thirdly, the
sifting among all the nations reveals the universal
dispersion of God's people. Fourthly, the chaff and
dust will be done away and lost. And finally, the
kernels, the true remnant of Israel, will be preserved
and delivered. The whole world is one great sieve
in which Israel is shaken from one place to another.
How vividly and accurately these words describe the
condition of Israel, especially since the destruction
of Jerusalem by the Romans in 70 A.D. Yet through
it all God has His eye on them to preserve them.
Only thus can their preservation in world-wide exile
and through age-long persecutions of the most diabolical sort, be explained. Note Luke 22:31 for a
process of sifting in the life of Peter. No grain falls

to the ground in this sifting of the Lord, but no sinner escapes either. All the sinners of the nation will perish; especially are those singled out who defiantly boasted that the evil judgment would not reach them. See 6: 3, the rich oppressors of Samaria. Those who did not believe in a judgment will be made to suffer it.

Restoration of David's Dynasty

At the end of Israel's sad dispersion He had promised to regather them and place over them His own righteous Ruler, the Messiah the son of David. Amos now foretells this in words of surpassing beauty. In the latter days of Israel's history the Lord will raise up the tabernacle (actually the hut or booth) of David that is fallen and in ruins; He will repair the breaches and ruins, building it as in the days of old. It is not a magnificent house of which the prophet speaks, but a ruined, fallen hut. This is in marked contrast to the splendid palace which David had erected for himself. II Samuel 5: 11, 12. The Davidic dynasty is usually referred to as "the house of David" as in II Samuel 3: 1; I Kings 11: 38; and Isaiah 7: 2, 13. In Isaiah 16: 5 we find the expression "the tent of David." In our Amos passage the low, degraded condition of the Davidic monarchy is meant. Isaiah 11: 1 also speaks of the lowly condition of the line of David. On the basis of this verse the rabbis of the Talmud called the Messiah, Bar Naphli ("the son of the fallen"), although Amos does not specifically mention the personal Messiah, only the line from which He was to come. Through David's Son the breaches of the Davidic house, the first of which it suffered upon the breaking away of

the ten tribes, will be repaired; the Davidic dynasty
and kingdom will be restored.   And the restoration
will be to its most glorious condition in the days of
old, that is, in the time of David and Solomon when
the kingdom was both undivided and prosperous,
enjoying in its full extent the greatest splendor of
kingly rule in all the history of Israel.   When Israel
has its rightful King on the throne, then it will be
the head of the nations.   Amos predicts that they will
possess the remnant of Edom, as well as all the nations that are called by the name of the Lord.   Mani-
festly the prophet is mentioning Edom as representative of all the nations of the world.   Most closely
related to Israel, they were the relentless foes of the
Lord's people.   See Obadiah 12.   The remnant that
is called by the name of the Lord is equivalent to
those designated in Joel 2: 32.   The citation of Amos
9: 11-12 by James in Acts 15 does not warrant us
in holding, as some do, that this prophecy is fulfilled
completely in this age of grace.   The phrase "in that
day" of our text refers to the last days of Israel.
The quotation of our verses in Acts 15: 16-18 is
made with one object in view: to confirm the fact of
the conversion of the Gentiles.   Hence the quotation
gives only the general sense of the Amos passage and
does not support the position that the Amos text has
in view the Christian Church as its ultimate fulfillment.   When Israel is head of the nations, their land
will be abundantly fruitful.   The one plowing will
overtake the reaper, and the treader of grapes the one
sowing seed.   The thought is that scarcely is the
farmer finished plowing when the seed will be ripe,
and hardly will he have completed treading the wine-

press when he will have to begin the sowing. Compare Leviticus 26: 5. Vintage time will continue to the sowing time because of the abundance of fruit. The mountains are said to drop with sweet wine, because vines are planted on the terraces of mountains. See Joel 3: 18 also. Israel will in that day be restored from centuries-long captivity to rebuild their cities and inhabit them with the enjoyment of their vineyards and gardens. Compare Hosea 6: 11 and contrast with 5: 11 of this book. Then Israel will be planted and rooted in their own land (II Samuel 7: 10), never more to be plucked up and uprooted from their God-given land. The day of exile, thank God, will be past. Note carefully Isaiah 61: 4; 62: 8, 9; 65: 21-23. How can these things be said to be true in our day when Israel knows only deportations (including those to the island of Cyprus) and not undisturbed settlement in her own land? Let us summarize the remarkable prophecy of Amos to be fulfilled in the consummation of Israel's history: (1) the restoration of the Davidic dynasty, verse 11; (2) the supremacy of Israel over the nations, verse 12; (3) the conversion of the nations, verse 12; (4) the fruitfulness of the land, verse 13; (5) the rebuilding of their cities, verse 14; and (6) their permanent settlement in their own land after their return from captivity, verse 15.

What of the Kernels?

God's heart is full of good things in store for Israel. What is the attitude of our hearts toward them? The chaff will be done away during Israel's world-wide sifting, but God has in mind the preservation of the

kernels. Even so now God has purposed the calling
out from Israel of those called "the remnant according to the election of grace." Romans 11: 5. But
nowhere in the Bible do we find that the remnant of
our day is to be preached to by another generation,
or that they are to be saved apart from the ministry
to them of the gospel of God's grace in His blessed
Son, the Messiah of Israel, our beloved Lord Jesus
Christ. Whether they be called remnant now or
kernels later, what of the lost ones in Israel whom
God wants for His glory? David's greater Son
awaits our faithfulness to His command to preach
to His own before He can come to take His Bride,
of redeemed Jews and Gentiles, to be with Himself
forever. And the time is this very present hour.

QUESTIONS ON CHAPTER IX

1. Of what does the last vision of the book speak?

2. Show the extent of the judgment indicated.

3. How does the prophet prove there will be no
escape?

4. Is the truth of the omnipresence of God viewed
alike by the godly and the wicked?

5. What nation is the instrument of God for judgment through this Book of Amos? Is it mentioned
by name?

6. How does the prophet bring out the omnipotence of God?

7. Does election ever provide a safeguard against
the wrath of God against sin?

8. What is the meaning of verse 7? Does it nullify
the promises to Abraham in Genesis 12: 1-3?

9. Do the Scriptures ever indicate that Israel, be-

cause she has been privileged of God, is saved by that fact alone?

10. How does the prophet prove that God is the God of all nations?

11. Will God destroy the entire house of Jacob?

12. What is promised the nation?

13. Explain fully the figure of the grain and the sieve.

14. What promise is set forth regarding the Davidic dynasty? Elaborate the prediction in its details.

15. Discuss the citation of this prophecy in Acts 15.

16. How is the prosperity of the land pictured? Will this be fulfilled literally?

17. Summarize the outstanding features of this prophecy in verses 11-15.

18. Will the remnant of our day be called out by another generation? Who is to give them the gospel now?

19. Are the kernels the same group of saved ones as the remnant according to the election of grace?

20. Shall we obey God and give Israel the gospel now?

OBADIAH:
DOOM UPON EDOM

Chapter I

GOD'S WRATH ON EDOM

The Prophet and His Times

THE prophecy of Obadiah is the smallest book
in the Old Testament, containing a total of but
twenty-one verses. It is not quoted in the New Testament, yet its message is a vital part of all the prophetic Scriptures. It is written in lucid and forceful
language. Nothing is known of Obadiah but his
name which means "servant of Jehovah." A number
of men in the Old Testament bore the same name.
There has been great diversity of opinion as to the
time of the prophecy. The enmity of Edom for
Israel was so unremitting and persistent through the
centuries that students of the book find it difficult to
assign the book to a specific time. Some estimates
have varied as much as approximately six centuries.
In all probability Obadiah was a prophet living before the Babylonian exile who foresaw by the Spirit
of prophecy the doom of Edom, the greatest enemy
of God's people, Israel. Compare Jeremiah 49: 7-22
for a later prophecy on the same subject which has
many verbal similarities with the prediction now be-

fore us. If Hosea treats of the love of God for Israel,
Amos of the righteousness of the Lord, Joel of the
Day of Jehovah, Obadiah prophesies of the doom of
Edom. The Edomites came from Esau, the twin
brother of Jacob. The Book of Genesis outlines in
unmistakable language the enmity that existed between these brothers. Their progeny perpetuated
this feud. Edom early became a powerful nation.
See Genesis 36; Exodus 15:15; Numbers 20:14ff.
When Israel came up from the land of Egypt, the
Edomites denied them passage through their land.
Note Numbers 20:20, 21. However, God commanded Israel to treat Edom as a brother. Deuteronomy 23:7, 8. Nevertheless, the hatred of Edom
(who well typifies the flesh and its desires with no
thought for the things of the spiritual life) persisted
against Israel, as the Old Testament Scriptures
abundantly attest. Now it is given to Obadiah to
pronounce God's message of final doom upon this
incorrigible foe of His people. The prophecy, though
centuries old, has a familiar ring, for it echoes events
and deeds of recent years that have been perpetrated
upon the sons of Jacob throughout the world.

The Pride and Fall of Edom

The prophecy begins with the concise statement
that it is a supernatural revelation, a vision, granted
to Obadiah; the word of the Lord that came to him
concerned Edom specifically. The prophet and the
nation Israel are made cognizant of the fact that the
Lord has sent a messenger among the nations to stir
them up to war against Edom. It is made known to
them by God directly, for He takes His own into His

plans for them and those about them. It was God's
overruling providences that led the Assyrians and
then Nebuchadnezzar with his confederates against
Edom. The Lord says of Edom that He has made
her small among the nations and greatly despised,
indeed, He speaks this word to her directly. God's
resolution to do so makes the humiliation as certain
as if it had already taken place. It will be accomplished through the enemies aroused against her.
What causes the fall of Edom? Her unbearable
pride. Her pride and conceit were nourished by the
fact that her land was full of high mountain fastnesses.
She truly dwelt in the clefts of the rock, for the land
of Edom is a rocky mountain full of caves and dwellings hewn out of the rock. The former inhabitants
of Mount Seir were troglodytes (cave-dwellers), the
Horites. See Genesis 14:6; Deuteronomy 2:12,
22. The haughty spirit of Edom evidently stemmed
from her belief that she was invincible and impreg-
nable. No one, she thought, could bring her down
from her lofty habitation. God assures her that,
though she emulate the eagle and though she set her
abode among the very stars, He will cast her down
thence. Compare Amos 9:2; Isaiah 14:12-20 (the
fall of Lucifer); Job 39:27, 28. Edom may be inac-
cessible to man, but not to God. The greater her
pride the more disastrous her fall.

Destruction and Treachery

The prophet sets forth now the thoroughgoing character of the destruction of the Idumeans. If robbers
break in at night, they steal all they need or can
carry away. They do not take all. When grape-

gatherers harvest the vintage, they always leave
gleanings as a matter of course. The vineyard is not
left completely bare. But, says Obadiah as he inter-
jects an exclamation of surprise and amazement at
the plundered condition of Edom, the land of Esau
will be left with nothing. Her ruin will be complete.
The enemy in seeking plunder will search out the
hidden treasures of Edom. The capital of Edom,
Petra, was the great market of the Syrian and Ara-
bian trade where many costly articles were treasured.
These will all be looted. Moreover, their own confederates will deceive them and prevail against them.
As a recompense for their treachery, their allies will
drive them out into captivity, let alone give them aid
in the hour of their need. The ones who had in
other days' enjoyed the bounty, the bread of Edom,
will employ treachery to bring about her certain
downfall. The Edomites will be able to look to no
one for help. By open means or deceptive snares
those who were their allies would compass their un-
doing. Esau will manifest none of that discernment
for which he had been renowned. The wise men of
the Mount of Esau will be destroyed. Because of its
communication with Babylon and Egypt and because
of the information gleaned through the caravans going to and from Europe and India, Edom had gained
an enviable reputation for wisdom. Now their wisdom will be withdrawn from them. The wise and
powerful men of Teman will be dismayed, because the
Lord purposed to slaughter every one in Edom. It
was to be a stroke without mitigation. For the wisdom of Teman see Job 4:1 and Jeremiah 49:7.

The Reasons for the Judgment

Such condign punishment calls for a presentation
of the underlying causes for the wrath of God against
Edom. Verses 10 through 14 give us the bill of particulars against this stubborn enemy of Israel. They
portray conditions in Israel when Judah was invaded
by Nebuchadnezzar. Edom resorted to violence
against his brother Jacob. Compare Joel 3:19. It
was directed against Jacob, his twin brother. There
were to be two phases to their punishment: (1) a
period in which they were to be a captive people—
shame covering them; (2) a time in which they
were to become extinct as a people. They were ultimately reduced by John Hyrcanus of the Maccabean
dynasty and lost their national existence under the
Romans. They were cut off for ever as a nation,
though the land would again be populated, as we
shall see from the latter part of this prophecy. When
the Chaldeans invaded Judah in later years, Edom,
like the enemies of God's people, had assumed an
attitude of hostility. Judah's goods were carried
off; her cities were entered by force; lots were cast
upon Jerusalem (Joel 3:3) to sell her population
into slavery; but Edom knew only hatred for her
kin, entering into the calamity as one of the accom-
plices of the outrages. For the hatred of Edom in
this hour see Psalm 137:7; 83:4-6 especially; Ezekiel 35; Jeremiah 49; Isaiah 34 and 63. In addi-
tion, Edom feasted on his brother's disaster and re-
joiced in the destruction of Judah, when he was
exiled as an alien from his homeland. Not only did
they revel in the calamity of Judah, but they used
arrogant language in exultation over their conquered

enemy. The Idumeans went from looks and rejoic-
ings to insults and actions. They assisted in the spoil-
ation of God's people when they were being robbed
by the invaders. Finally, they took their stand at
the crossway to cut off the retreat of those who
wanted to pass through Idumea to Egypt where they
were fleeing from the Chaldean hosts, and then delivered them over to the enemy. They surely compounded their outrages against the distressed ones of
Jacob. Note the extent of them: (1) violence, verse
10; (2) hostile attitude, verse 11; (3) joy at
Israel's calamity, verse 12; (4) boasting in Jacob's
time of distress, verse 12; (5) spoiling of God's
people, verse 13; (6) prevention of the escape of
the fugitives, verse 14; and (7) the betrayal of them
into the hand of their enemy, verse 14. Should not
the Lord take account of this? His wrath is kindled
with reason. Edom has merited her punishment.

The Day of Jehovah at Hand

Dwelling on the theme of God's visitation in
wrath, Obadiah is carried on in mind and heart by
the Spirit of God to the great day of judgment for
all nations. In God's reckoning the day of the Lord
is near for all the nations who have similarly mal-
treated the people of God. They will, as Edom, be
requited in kind. Edom will come in for judgment
in the day of the Lord. As the seed of Esau have
held their wild carousals with the conquerors in the
captured city of Jerusalem in their time, so shall all
these nations drain to the dregs the cup of calamity
and wrath of God. See Jeremiah 25: 15-33. In so
doing they shall be so completely annihilated, that it

will be as though they had never existed. The time
of this judgment will be just before the establish-
ment of Messiah's kingdom; then the power of Edom
will be finally and completely broken. When the
last great confederacy against Israel takes place
(Zechariah 12: 1ff.; 14: 1ff.), the Edomites will be
among these adversaries of God's people. They will
be routed and Edom will be blotted out as a nation.
When other nations, like Assyria and Egypt, are
restored and brought into millennial blessing, Edom
will have been utterly destroyed. Edom, representative of the flesh and the carnal mind with its enmity
against God and His law, must be irrevocably cut off.

Israel's Salvation and Messiah's Kingdom

Whereas Edom can only expect destruction in the
wind-up of God's prophetic program, Israel awaits
a restoration from world-wide captivity. In Mount
Zion will be those of Israel who have escaped the
rigors and ravages of the centuries of cruel treatment
accorded this people of God. They will be resettled
upon their own land. Mount Zion, so often polluted
by the repeated invasions of the foreigner, will be
holy unto the Lord. Compare Isaiah 52: 1. The
house of Jacob will then possess their possessions;
they will fully occupy those provinces and countries
which were theirs in the time of the greatest expansion of the monarchy in Israel. She will no longer
be shorn of her possessions. Then Israel, before
this the butt of every attack, will be God's instrument
in punishing Edom. Note Isaiah 11: 14; Zechariah
12: 6. The houses of Jacob and Joseph, the reunited
kingdoms, will be as fire to stubble when they execute
9

God's wrath in the last days upon an Edom revived
in prophetic times for this very judgment. No remnant is specified for Edom from this judgment. All
will be cut off. Then Israel will regain the territories
that rightfully belong to her. Those who dwell in
the southern portion of Judah will appropriate to
themselves Mount Esau; those of the lowlands on the
west will gain the land of the Philistines. The territory of the northern kingdom will be restored and
enjoyed; and Benjamin, loyal to the Davidic dynasty,
will expand to the east to Gilead. We have here a
fulfillment of Genesis 28: 14. The large number of
Israelitish captives in Phoenicia (where they had
been sold and from there into Greece) will possess
the land to Zarephath, a town between Sidon and
Tyre near the shore of the Mediterranean, the
Sarepta of Luke 4: 26. The Judean captives in
Sepharad will gain the cities of the south mentioned
in verse 19. What is the identity of Sepharad? It
has never been satisfactorily identified. Conjectures
range from Spain (so the Aramaic versions and the
rabbis), the Bosphorus (the position held by the
Latin translator of the Bible, Jerome), Saparda in
southwest Media according to many, Sparta, and
Sardis. The important truth is that Judah and
Israel respectively will possess the land adjoining
them. And then saviours, deliverers and rulers like
the early judges in Israel during the days of the
theocracy when God ruled His people directly, will
ascend Mount Zion to judge, to punish, the Mount
of Esau, and the kingdom shall be Jehovah's—blessed
consummation. See Judges 3: 9, 15. These deliverers
will exercise authority in the name of the Lord, but

ultimate sovereignty will be His alone. Read carefully Daniel 2:44; Zechariah 14:9; Luke 1:33; Revelation 19:6; and especially Psalm 22:28 for the wording. To recapitulate the salient features of this important prophecy: Obadiah in pre-exilic days sees by the Spirit of God the culmination of Edom's hatred for Israel in her vicious conduct toward the distraught people in the day of their exile by Nebuchadnezzar. The prophet traces the sources of this attitude and pictures vividly the features of the punishment of God upon Edom for her attitudes, arrogant speech, and actions. When is the time of the fulfillment of this prophecy? The fulfillment of the ruin of Edom foretold by Obadiah was begun in the Chaldean period. Edom was laid waste by them, Jeremiah 49:7ff. and Ezekiel 35. The Maccabees further subjugated them. The Romans completed their ruin at the time that they destroyed Jerusalem in 70 A.D. Through these centuries we hear nothing of Edom. In the end time and before the gathering of the nations against Jerusalem in the Battle of Armageddon, Edom will again be on the scene of world history. There is to be revival of many ancient nations. See Luke 21:29, especially the words "and all the trees." Then Edom will experience to the full the wrath of God in destruction, the Lord Jesus Christ Himself executing the judgment of God on Edom and her allies. Isaiah 63:1-6. With the wicked nations destroyed and Edom cut off, Israel restored from captivity will possess all the land originally promised by God to Abraham and the Lord will reign over the earth.

Learn from Edom!

What shall we learn from Edom? We can learn, first, the displeasure, unspeakable and abiding, of God on those who treat Israel ill; and the pleasure of God to establish the kingdom of His dear Son on Mount Zion over restored and converted Israel. Let us hasten that glad and consummating day by evangelizing Israel to a finish!

QUESTIONS ON OBADIAH

1. Indicate the place of the Book of Obadiah among the books of the Old Testament.

2. What do we know of the man Obadiah?

3. What is the theme of the prophecy?

4. Can we date the book as to the time of the events narrated in it? Give reasons for your answer.

5. Outline briefly the history of the conflict between Edom and Israel.

6. What means does God use for the overthrow of Edom?

7. What is the great and chief sin of Edom?

8. How was this sin sponsored by the natural site of Edom?

9. How does Obadiah picture the extent of the destruction of Esau's land?

10. Will Edom's wisdom avail in the hour of judgment? Explain.

11. What are the underlying causes for the wrath of God against this nation?

12. What phases of judgment are set forth for Edom?

13. Enumerate the outrages of Edom against the people of God.

14. Why is the Day of the Lord introduced in verse 15?

15. Fit Edom's doom and judgment into the prophetic scheme of the Bible for the last days of Israel's age.

16. Will Edom ever recover from her judgment as Assyria and Egypt will?

17. Outline the features of Israel's restoration as set forth by Obadiah.

18. What is meant by Sepharad?

19. Who are the "saviours" mentioned in the last verse of the book?

20. Summarize the entire prophecy of Obadiah.

21. What can the nations of the earth learn from Edom? Explain fully.

22. What can we as children of God learn?

23. Can you show that the evangelization of Israel brings the hour of God's consummation of all things nearer?

24. Is there time for delay?

INDEX OF SUBJECTS

INDEX OF SCRIPTURE REFERENCES

Printed in the USA
CPSIA information can be obtained
at www.ICGtesting.com
LVHW021104131023
760943LV00005B/104